NOT YOUR TYPICAL PASTOR'S WIFE

NOT YOUR TYPICAL PASTOR'S WIFE

SOMETIMES THINGS ARE JUST PLAIN FUNNY!

JUDY GIDDENS SHERIFF, PH.D.

Copyright © 2018 Judy Giddens Sheriff
ISBN 978-1-938796-55-5 (soft cover)
Library of Congress Control Number 2018954837

Edited by
Jeannette DiLouie, Innovative Editing

Cover Illustration by
Blueberry Illustrations

Interior Design by
Candy Abbott

Published by
Fruitbearer Publishing LLC
P.O. Box 777, Georgetown, DE 19947
302.856.6649 • FAX 302.856.7742
www.fruitbearer.com • info@fruitbearer.com

Printed in the United States of America

To my husband,
whose ministry allows me to enjoy
a life of happiness, fulfillment,
and humorous experiences.
My love for him is endless.

To the friends whose encouragement
prompted me to write about my experiences
as a pastor's wife so that I could bring
moments of laughter and happiness to others.

To God with thanks and praise
for making me in His image and blessing me
with a keen sense of humor and a million or
more reasons to laugh and smile!

Contents

Chapter 1

It's Nobody

When I made the call, a child answered the phone. Identifying myself, I asked to speak to her mother, only to hear her yell at the top of her lungs, "Mom, telephone!" After regaining my hearing, I heard the parent ask who it was; and again, the voice screamed, "It's nobody! Just the preacher's wife!"

The thought of hanging up the phone crawled through my mind as I glanced in a nearby mirror to get a look at this "nobody" and see if I had, indeed, been diminished to nothingness. Physically, I was still there. But the experience stirred up a desire to take a long look at who I really am in the eyes of the public and our parishioners, and especially God.

Before I begin showing you the real me that came to light, I must give you some very important background information that might help you understand this author. As I was stretched across my bed thinking about my life, thoughts swirled above me like dust strings on a ceiling fan. Ideas and experiences began to pounce in my mind like a hound dog going after a pile of chicken bones.

I knew it was time to tell my story.

I come from a long line of preachers. It's in my blood. My mother's father was a preacher. My daddy's father was a preacher. I have several uncles who are preachers. And if I ever delved further into my ancestry, I'd probably find more.

Maybe that's why, back in college, I mostly dated ministerial students. I never could understand a better reason when I was too flighty and fun-loving to ever consider settling into the role of being a preacher's wife should any of those relationships take a turn toward the serious. I loved a good belly laughter joke or story, and I could keep up with the best of them when it came to sharing the funny things of life. It seemed I was never serious until my grades came out. Then I'd be forced to realize I had belly-laughed my way right into college summer school.

With that said, I grew up in a Christian home, where my parents instilled some wonderful values in me. Those values stayed with me through my growing-up years and on into college and beyond. I'm very thankful for my parents and what they taught me, which helped me through so much. At times, with peer pressure and feeling like I was being pulled in multiple directions like warm taffy, so many of my Mother's wise words would echo in my head.

As such, I could always see her facial expressions when I knew I wasn't making good decisions: a look like she was wearing shoes two sizes too small. I knew that look — it was the same one she'd give me when I was a child sitting in the pew, misbehaving in church. She was in the choir, and when I'd glance at her, she'd be wearing that same expression that told me I either had to straighten up or the wrath of that woman was my fate.

Some people said I was probably as spoiled as two-week old 'tater salad because I was an only child. But I really wasn't. I knew how to share, and I did. If I wanted to purchase something, I did my chores and earned my weekly $0.25 allowance. And when I saved enough money, I would purchase my item.

I truly had a wonderful family and childhood.

College was a new experience for me, naturally, but I loved every minute of it. Again, I have no idea why I was drawn like a fly to honey to the ministerial guys. They, for the most part, were very serious-minded, while I wasn't. And they seemed to have their heads on straight, knowing what they wanted in life—while I didn't. We mixed like oil and water, yet I kept accepting dates nonetheless. As a much older and wiser adult, I can look back and see where God was preparing me for my future—and to be a preacher's wife after all. Though, back then, if someone had told me that I really would become such a thing, my stomach would have twisted like a string mop in a bucket.

No way did I ever see myself marrying a preacher! I just wasn't "preacher wife material." Loved to date 'em, sure, but didn't want to marry 'em. That was probably my college dating motto. Oh, I'm sure I had to kiss a lot of preacher frogs before my prince finally came along.

I often wondered about my personality and why I always laughed so much and found so much in life to be funny. After giving it much thought, I realized that it came from my Mother's side of the family. When they got together, they would sit up all night telling stories about their childhood, laughing uncontrollably as they did. It didn't matter if they had just come from a funeral where a loved one was buried; they would always find ways to enjoy being together.

I inherited that same sense of humor, making my mother and me a dangerous combination together—when I wasn't misbehaving alone in the church pew, of course. Many times, my Daddy had to separate us in church or in the choir or wherever there was a gathering and we were sitting side by side. Even our music director at the church would have to call us by name and ask us to separate.

Our times together were wonderful.

I remember so well one Sunday morning in particular. We had a dear friend who was going to be baptized. And while we knew he'd been injured in a war and had severe hearing damage, that was the extent of what we knew about his military experiences. Mother and I sat beside each other in the choir (big mistake) and waited as the organist played softly.

We heard the baptismal waters being stirred, and we all turned to watch the preacher walk down into the baptistery first, then hold out his hand. Yet as our friend walked into the water, we couldn't help but notice how he had sandwich bags tied around each ear. Clearly, we weren't the only ones to catch that detail since another lady in the choir — who couldn't whisper quietly — said, "Oh, my Lord, he's got baggies on his ears."

Well, that did it. Mother and I got hysterical. I really did turn as far as I could so she wouldn't be in my peripheral vision. But I could hear her snickering, and that made it worse. My daddy gave us both the "evil eye," which didn't help a bit either. I didn't think we'd ever get our composure.

In my defense, I toyed with the idea of slipping down in my seat and crawling out the side door of the choir loft. But then I remembered a time when our little 80-pound, almost 100-year old organist tried such a stunt. During prayers, she came crawling into the choir loft to hand someone a piece of music. All things considered, including how the congregation had their heads bowed, many people didn't see her entrance. Yet when she tried to crawl back out to the side door, she forgot it was a short swinging door. When she tried to hoist herself up, the door swung open and out she rolled onto the rostrum.

After that vision popped into my head, I decided not to try crawling out. I'd just have to endure the baptism and wait for Daddy's reprimand.

Sometime later, the pastor admitted to Daddy that he was doing just fine that day until he saw our friend walk into the water with sandwich bags on his ears. "I didn't dare look at Judy or her mother," was how he put it.

We were well-known for our humorous personalities, to say the least. Most of my family and friends know this about me: If I get tickled and am laughing until I cry, it's pointless to ask me to straighten up or be quiet. That's like adding fuel to the fire. They understand to just leave me alone and let it run its course. I'll be fine when it does—sometimes.

Laughter is just a big part of who I am. Which should make it clearer why I'm nobody's prim and proper idea of a preacher's wife. There seems to be no serious bone in my body.

Chapter 2

A Pastor's Wife

Isn't it amusing how things are always funnier in church or at a funeral or any place where you're supposed to be composed and dignified? No? Is it just me?

Regardless, another one of my clearest memories growing up was of a great friend of mine who had a beautiful voice and could play the piano to perfection. She and I sang together many times and always had a wonderful time in the process. Because our voices blended so well, we'd been asked to sing at my grandmother's church where a visiting minister would be preaching the evening service. Accepting, we planned out our music and arrangement: She would play the piano and sing, and I'd stand beside her and sing.

Depending on the occasion, we might have someone else play for us. But on this particular night, that wasn't the case, which was fine. Everything was going just great right down to our attire, which we coordinated so we wouldn't clash or look like a fruit bowl had thrown up — you know, with flowers, stripes, and weird designs. In short, we wanted to have that more "conservative" look. So it was light blue skirts and somewhat matching tops for the two of us.

We decided to sit in the front row to make it easier to get up to sing when the time came. But first came the sermon, which was captivating. The preacher expounded on the Gospel, talking about the Alpha and Omega. We were totally taken with his message — until he said something that made my ears perk up: "The Alfalfa and Omega."

He said it more than once, too.

It was far too funny for my own good. Nudging my friend, I leaned over and whispered as inconspicuously as possible, "Did you hear what he said?"

She had a beautiful smile and gorgeous white teeth, and when she looked at me, she broke out in a grin so big I could practically see every tooth in her mouth. First, her shoulders started shaking, and then I could hear the giggles start to slip out.

For my part, I was already in a terrible fix with no place to run. Our careful foresight for perfect placement meant we were in the front row right under the preacher's nose. That left me with little recourse every time he mentioned "the Alfalfa" but to pray under my breath, "Oh please, Lord, make him stop."

The Lord chose not to answer that prayer with an immediate yes. In fact, He let it get worse from there.

Unable to keep Mother Nature at bay, my friend finally couldn't hold it any longer. She nudged me to whisper, "I've wet my pants!" Of course, that was right about when we knew the preacher was winding down and it was almost time for us to get up and sing.

"What am I going to do?" She kept whispering. "I can't get up there like this. My skirt is wet!"

Well, me, being the genius I am, very calmly said, "Turn your skirt around during the prayer, and no one will know."

So, sure enough, during the prayer and before we got up to sing the invitational hymn, she quickly turned her skirt around.

That took care of the problem while we walked up to sing with our backs to the congregation. The dry part of her skirt was facing them.

But then she turned around to face everyone, and that's when I saw the biggest mistake I'd made in a long time. The big wet spot — once located in the back — was now turned around. At my insistence. For the whole church to see.

Staring at it, not a note would come out of my mouth.

That's when I did another terrible thing. Completely unable to sing, I instead pretended to be "spiritually moved," making my way down the steps to the altar. While my friend stood there in all her drenched glory, I was at the altar laughing my head off.

Afterward, I did have to ask the Lord to forgive me for pretending to be so moved by the sermon and the Spirit. But every time I hear a preacher talk about the Alpha and Omega, I recall that night and I laugh all over again.

Can you blame me?

I am indeed my mother's child, and I'm proud of it. Things are just funny to us that probably aren't funny to anyone else.

My mother had faith in me that I would one day learn to somewhat control myself, though I never did. And neither did she. We continued to laugh together right up to the time she went into a diabetic coma at the age of 89 and went home to be with the Lord—the very One who gave her that precious personality.

I know she would want me to continue with my sense of humor down here on earth. And I can't disobey my parent, now, can I? So, the laughter continues in my life.

She did live long enough to see me become a preacher's wife, and I'm sure there were times she wondered if I could handle it. But she knew me well, including how my sense of humor was just part of me—and that no amount of nudging, begging, or bribing me would ever stop my laughter.

Thinking about this, I had to do a little brain-recalling and try to remember the preachers' wives I was familiar with while growing up. I wanted to see if I "measured up."

My first recollection was of our pastor when I was just a young child. He was probably close to six and a half feet tall: a giant in this little girl's eyes. His wife, meanwhile, was around five feet tall. With her high heels on.

She played the organ during the worship service, was very quiet and soft-spoken, and pretty much stayed in the background in general. I'm sure she was a great wife to her Goliath of a husband and a good mother to their three sons, who I was sure came from the darkest pits of the earth. Back then, I was exceptionally frightened of them. It wasn't until later on that I learned they were just typical boys doing typical boy stuff, which included scaring the mud out of little girls.

To their credit, I must say all three turned out to be fine adults. Yet some of their antics as children could have sent me to therapy.

After several years serving as our pastor, Goliath was called to another church and ours began the search for a new pastor. That left me wondering what he would be like and what kind of wife he would have. As it so happened, he was technically single when he came around, though he promptly told the congregation he'd soon be married to a former missionary in Africa.

That, to my young mind, sounded really neat! I had seen pictures in magazines at church, so I felt like I was sort of familiar with the work. Yet "sort of" wasn't good enough, as it turned out. I wasn't at all prepared for this new person to enter our pastor's life and take charge of things.

For some reason, I was hoping for a beauty queen to come upon the scene, possibly wearing her tiara and robe. But was I wrong. Oh, the things a child's mind can conjure up.

The actual lady — not the figment of my imagination — was very nice but plain as an old shoe in the back of my closet. No makeup. Homely hairdo. Quiet. Reserved. And probably a bit apprehensive of her new life away from the jungles of Africa. That might have been why she didn't get involved in many things at the church.

She did, however, teach the young girls in G.A.'s. I was part of this group and, as time went on, I began to notice she wore makeup and styled her hair much better in a short bob. She was really a nice lady, but she didn't laugh a lot and she certainly didn't double over with belly laughs like I did and still do.

Even so, as I grew up further, I learned to appreciate her quiet spirit, no matter how I wasn't directly influenced by it.

Sometimes, even now, I wish I could be more like her in that respect. But that's not the case. I am who God made me to be!

By the time I became a college student, another new pastor arrived on the scene in our little town. He'd received his education in Scotland and had a bit of an accent, which I thought so unique. Plus, he had a wonderful personality and was full of wit. As such, the thought struck me like a squirt gun to the eye that he must have a great wife! She surely had to have a wonderful personality like his, and no doubt she'd be one to laugh and tell funny stories. She could probably do the bend-over-belly-laugh thing, too!

Nope. No witty pastor's wife. No wife, at all. Apparently, this pastor was single as well, though engaged to a lady from Kentucky. Sure enough, they married and came back to our little town where the church had a reception so we all could meet this new addition to our congregation.

Growing up, I loved the *Popeye* cartoon, and this preacher's wife was Olive Oyle's twin! In my young-adult college eyes, she just didn't match up with him. But they were happy, so I accepted "Mrs. Oyle" as our preacher's wife and soon found her to be quite charming. No, she didn't laugh like a hyena or lose her breath chortling at a story or joke like I did, but she was our preacher's wife and we learned to love her just as we loved him.

After having dated ministerial students in college and an employed preacher after college, not to mention seeing all the wives of my past preachers, you would think I'd just go on my merry way and see where it led. God had so many ideas for me, and I knew that. But this was one I knew all on my own: I would *never* be a preacher's wife.

I wonder how hard God laughs when we make statements like that.

Believe it or not, my mother had a hand in my becoming a preacher's wife. "If it was the Lord's will," she would say. She never came out and admitted it, but I suppose she saw potential in me that I didn't. So she was delighted when her good friend called to tell her about a young visiting preacher who'd be filling in at their church in another county. And wouldn't it be a great idea if I met him?

At that time, their church didn't have a pastor, so they had seminary students coming in to fill the pulpit as needed. My mother's friend explained how, for whatever reason, she'd inquired about this particular young man, seen his picture and thought him to be quite handsome. This got my fun-loving mother intrigued, setting us up for yet another kind of situation where we couldn't have been serious no matter how hard we tried.

With much persuasion on Mother's part, I agreed to go. My daddy was a Gideon speaker, and it just so happened that he was speaking at a church in another town that Sunday. So Mother and I decided to go meet this "mystery man" on our own. By then, I was out of college, teaching school, and beginning to get my life in order.

But I still didn't want to marry a preacher.

Even so, I drove to Mother's house, picked her up and off we went into the country about twenty miles away. Because my mother was a Southern woman through and through — which meant wearing white gloves, hats, and dressing to the nines — we were quite gussied up. I did persuade her to let me omit the hat, but she got her way in insisting I wear her fur stole.

"It looks so elegant and Southern and lady-like," she told me.

Admittedly, it was in the late fall and the weather did require some type of wrap. Plus, the brown rabbit fur did genuinely look nice. It's just that she failed to realize how it had been packed away for a very long time. I didn't want to meet this young man smelling like mothballs, but I ended up reluctantly agreeing to bring it with me.

Putting the stole in the backseat of my car, we chattered happily the whole time about this apparently cute young preacher. To me, if it all panned out, it would possibly lead to some dates. To Mother, it would lead right to a wedding, which she was already planning.

The conversation was fun and light-hearted from start to finish.

When we arrived, however, it was evident how my fur stole was going to be really out of place. Walking up the walkway, I immediately saw that there were two screen doors at the front of the building. Not that surprising. This was, after all, out in the country and they probably didn't have air conditioning. In the summer, they probably just opened the doors to let the breeze come through the screens.

I was okay with that until I got closer and saw "Merita Bread Company" stamped in faded paint across those screens. It just struck me as funny, and I was so tickled I could hardly tell Mother to look. When I did manage to get the words out, she saw it and became hysterical herself, leading to the two of us standing there in the yard, laughing like two lunatics with our legs crossed to avoid any unfortunate accidents.

Entertained as we were, we knew we had to go in when her friend was expecting us. We really did try to get our composure together, but just when we thought we'd accomplished it, I reached for the screen door, which was shut over the regular door behind it.

Screeeeech!

I tell you, nowhere in this world has there ever been a door that made as much noise as this one did, setting me right back off. Laughing all over again, I let it close as gently as I could. Which wasn't nearly gently enough.

Scronnnnnch!

By that time, Mother had reached for the other door, causing the same sound to belt out. If we could have fanned the two doors back and forth, we could have probably played "Dixie." Oh, excuse me. We were at church. So we could have played, "When the Roll is Called Up Yonder, I'll Be There."

We genuinely didn't know what to do. Church was beginning, and there we stood on the steps, playing our musical screen doors, with me draped in my rabbit fur stole ready to meet Mr. Wonderful.

We were saved when an usher opened the main door. And then the screen door, too.

Screeeech!

The two of us walked into the vestibule looking like the happiest creatures alive. Our faces were nothing but huge smiles while as we tried to hold back our laughter.

The usher escorted us to our seats in the second row of the middle pews since the church was rather full. Mother let me be ushered in front of her, but before we got there, I heard her giggling as I paraded down the aisle — unaware of the new situation brewing behind me. When we were both appropriately seated, I turned to her.

"What was so funny? Are you still thinking about those screen doors?"

"No," she whispered back. "Give me your fur stole."

I gave her an odd look.

"I'll explain later."

I couldn't imagine why she wanted the thing after she'd made such a big deal about me wearing it. Yet she was getting tickled all over again, so I did as requested, watching while she very gently folded it and laid it beside her in the pew.

Mother's friend was playing the organ that day, but she didn't look happy up there. She kept shooting glances our way with an expression that told me her girdle was way too tight. It was a peculiarly painful look that made me both curious and sympathetic.

I kept looking for the preacher while we sang a few songs, yet no one in the front pews even closely resembled a young seminary student. As it turned out, the individual in question was waiting behind a side door to make his appearance at the pulpit area.

When he did, he positively crept in.

The pastor that met my gaze was old—extremely so!—with very little hair. And it took forever for him to lift his Bible to the pulpit. Moreover, after speaking only a few words, his very long and wide tongue flew out of his mouth like a frog catching a fly.

Dear heavens above! Nobody has a tongue that long!

Nobody but him, that was. He continued to do that same tongue-thing after each phrase until I was downright mesmerized and began counting how many times he could have caught a fly. Coming back to reality at some point, my heart plummeted. If this organist friend of Mother's wanted me to meet THIS MAN, then she was crazier than a bed bug high on Pixy Stix!

We managed to get through the sermon and the remainder of the service without any overt laughter or panic attacks. But apparently, we weren't the only ones fixated on something other than the sermon the whole time. Afterward, Mother's friend came flying over to where we stood.

"I know you think I told you a story," she fretted. "I didn't know the young seminary student had called and canceled until right before church, and then there was nothing I could do to let you know. I saw your expressions and felt so bad for Judy!"

With that explanation taken care of, we all had a good laugh at my expense, with another good giggle to come.

As we left the church, I asked Mother what was so funny when we were walking in, which made her burst out laughing all over again. With good reason.

My eyes got big as salad plates when she held the stole up

for me to see!

According to her, every time I took a step, the accessory would slide further down and down until it was underneath my rump, giving me that full-skirt look. That might not have been utterly awful except that, to top it all off, the fur had dry-rotted without us realizing it, and clumps of fur kept falling down the aisle. All I had left when I got to the pew was a rabbit skin.

"I tried to kick the clumps of fur under the pews," she said, which brought about yet another vivid mental image. She must have resembled a very old flower girl in a wedding, tossing out rose petals — except that she was kicking fur balls around.

Oh. My. Goodness.

Just another way of showing how I wasn't cut out to be a preacher's wife.

Chapter 3

Never a Dull Moment

Many years have passed since those college and post-graduation days, and I've experienced many things in life. Some of them were devastating. Some were happy and fulfilling. And some have left me wondering what to do next.

Others just make me realize exactly how big God's sense of humor really can be.

I know this for a variety of reasons, including how He sometimes brings us to places where we have to eat our words. Big time.

Despite the numerous times I declared I'd never become a preacher's wife, here I am today with a grin bigger than a Moon Pie and thinking how very blessed I am that God gave me a preacher for a husband. Who would have thought it could possibly become a reality? Certainly not this old girl! Yet it worked out so beautifully.

It's not always so easy to see how beautiful life's unexpected events can be, of course. Looking back, I can see a whole string of experiences tagging along behind me, clinging to my memory, and sometimes prompting questions like, "God, are You sure this is for me?"

When my husband answered the call to his first church as pastor, we really didn't know what to expect. I wondered if the people would like us. Would they accept us? And just maybe, might I be about to make some wonderful new friends? It didn't take long before we knew it was going to be a sweet congregation and that we'd fall in love with all of them.

It also didn't take long before we were falling into our roles. As it so happened, they didn't just need a pastor; they also needed someone to help with the bulletins since they didn't have a church secretary to keep a church office open and active.

So naturally, being the new kid on the block, I politely offered my services to print and fold, completely clueless that it would evolve into being the official church secretary.

The church also asked if I could help with the music. Since I had always sung in a church choir, not to mention my college choir, I just assumed they meant they needed some more people to sing. So, again, I said yes, only to find out they were thinking more along the lines of me leading worship and directing the choir for good.

After that, I thought they were possibly through asking the new preacher's wife to step into roles they so desperately needed help with.

I was wrong.

Off to the side of the pulpit area sat an organ that evidently hadn't been played in quite a while. Sheepishly, someone asked, "Do you by any chance play the organ?"

Well, I couldn't tell a lie, so I answered in the affirmative, already knowing where this was headed. Sure enough, they all but shouted with happiness. In my mind, I could hear them saying, "Yippee! A packaged deal." There was the new preacher and there was the new preacher's wife who could automatically accept three hats: church secretary, music director, and organist.

Somewhere in there, of course, I was also supposed to wear the "wife hat," which made for some fascinating costume changes. Yet I learned to truly love all three jobs. And even though my "hats" would go on to become worn with age, I wouldn't trade them for anything in this world.

Back in the beginning, since we were new to the church, the members of course loved to stop by for chats to get to know us better. On one particular day, I was sitting at my desk when one of the elderly ladies came over to talk with the pastor. I showed her into Richard's office, and though I could hear them talking, I didn't know what they were saying. Nor was I trying to listen in.

I figured this was their personal time.

Soon enough, this dear little lady came back into my office, smiled, gave me a motherly hug, and left. That was when my husband came out as well to stand in the doorway, his face as white as freshly picked cotton. Beads of perspiration covered his face.

At a glance, I knew something was wrong. Did I need to call 9-1-1? He assured me he didn't need medical attention; he just needed to sit down and breathe. So I dutifully removed my secretary's hat and put on the wife hat instead to inquire about his situation.

I never dreamed it would be a story to go down in the annals of preacher history.

As his wife, I naturally wanted to know what had upset him so badly. However, when he told me, it was hard to stay entirely sympathetic. In short, I lost it laughing no matter how hard I tried to stay somber. This was one of those deep, bend-over belly-laughs that just couldn't be helped.

My poor husband didn't think it was all that funny, but I still chortle today when we talk about it. Bless this little old lady's dear heart. She was just trying to share her tale of woe with her new pastor, even if this particular one wasn't one he needed to hear.

It seems she had tried a feminine product she wasn't very familiar with that somehow managed to work its way into another part of her body, which then required medical attention at the emergency room in order to be removed.

Unlike her, I'll stop there. According to my husband, she went into full detail relaying it to him. And try as I'm sure he did, he couldn't find a Scripture to rectify that situation.

She meant no harm. That much was clear. And just as clearly, no harm was done — except to give the pastor a few nights of bad dreams.

He'd had his day — and survived! Now it was my turn.

Another dear saint dropped by to sit and talk with me. As I listened to her history of medical problems and offered my assurance of prayer for her, she surprised me with the news that she'd had a heart operation before. We talked on for a little while after that.

Then she decided it was show-and-tell time.

Now, my office had a big window in front of my desk. So anyone could see inside just as well as I could see outside. Plus, the pastor's office was right outside my own and he was there that day, studying. All was well until she felt the necessity to show me her scar.

See where this is going?

Like a flash, out came the blouse over her skirt! Up it went until it reached her chin, and her bra separated enough for her to show me the scar.

Oh please, dear sweet Jesus, don't let the preacher walk in on this!

That's what went through my mind. If he had, after his ordeal with the other member and her feminine product, I do believe he would have turned in his resignation. Either that or get committed to an institution. He'd never heard of any of his preacher friends having to deal with these kinds of things before.

With that great concern first and foremost in my mind, I jumped to my feet, ran around my desk, and proceeded to help her get her bra back in place and her blouse tucked back into her skirt. That was one of those times when I definitely thanked God for answering my prayer. My husband didn't walk in, and no one was in the parking lot to observe our show-and-tell session.

Like I said: God has a sense of humor, doesn't He?

By the time hubby had been in ministry there for a few years, it was safe to say that there always seemed to be something happening to make him wonder if God had really called him. Really, he was sure; but there were just some situations that needed to be handled by someone else. Someone other than him.

For example, a lady visited our church on a regular basis. She never actually became a member but enjoyed all the benefits of being one. In her defense, she did have many health issues. Yet they always manifested themselves at very inopportune times, particularly for my husband. Even though she wasn't a member, he was generally gracious enough to help however he could. That's just who he is. He has a heart of gold and is always ready to assist.

Well, almost always. There was this one exception.

When my phone rang in the office that day, I immediately recognized this woman's number on the caller ID and figured she wasn't calling for me. Sure enough, she asked to be put through to the pastor's office, and I made the connection as requested. Then I went about my business.

That goal admittedly got a little more difficult when I heard his voice grow a bit louder than usual, but, overall, I paid no attention to it until the conversation came to an end. When he entered my office and sat down in front of me, I already knew to expect something.

Oh, no. Another situation that requires the wife hat.

It certainly did, though I'm not sure how well I handled it. Like my husband, I'm all for helping anyone who genuinely needs a hand. And I'll go out of my way to do whatever I can to see that someone is properly taken care of. But even I knew this particular request was way beyond the call of duty on his part.

As the story came out, I tried to keep a straight face. But the giggles soon began to rise and, before I knew it, I was erupting into that same old belly laugh. This poor pastor of mine had truly been tossed into a sea of unfamiliarity, with the lady's request completely throwing him for a loop. I was so glad he'd been on the phone with her instead of sitting face-to-face in his office. I have no idea how that would have played out.

The request? She had been to the doctor for some medical reason and been prescribed medication as a result. She didn't go into detail on the original problem, but it seems the medication had caused her some constipation discomfort. And that, she *did* go into detail about.

This lady was a bit on the heavily plump side and had difficulty getting around, so we understood that trying to get to the pharmacy — or any store, for that matter — could be an issue for her. We also understood that she couldn't rely on her husband for help. That's why she depended on her "unofficial" pastor for assistance so very often.

But she pushed that charity a little too far that day when she boldly asked if he would go buy some suppositories for her and bring them to her house. I think that was about the time I heard his voice go up a few decibels. It's also when he told her in no uncertain terms that he most certainly would *not* do any such thing, suggesting that she let her husband take care of it instead.

"He's tired, and I don't want to disturb him," she explained.

"Then call your Sunday school teacher," her harried non-pastor said. "I'm not taking care of this for you."

The poor guy! Again, none of his preacher friends had ever been asked to purchase suppositories for their church members. And not one of his seminary studies had ever prepared him for this kind of thing. So it's entirely understandable that he sometimes wondered if God was trying to send him a different message than he'd originally believed.

Some days, I'll admit, I felt like my life was in the toilet, too, with vultures circling overhead. But then someone would call or come by for a visit, or something would happen to lift my spirits and make me smile and deeply satisfied that God had put us in the right place. Even situations like the ones mentioned, although disturbing — okay, downright shocking — at the time, have proven to provide smiles down the road as I recall some of my experiences as the preacher's wife.

Chapter 4

Life's Lemons and Apple Butter

"Funeral? What funeral? Who died?" Those were the questions I bombarded my husband with the day he walked into the kitchen and told me to hurry and get dressed for the funeral. But to properly understand this situation, you have to understand that it all had to do with apple butter.

Under the right inspiration, I love making apple butter; but it's one of those things I really have to be in the mood to do. When that mood strikes, there's no stopping me until everything is done. And that morning, when I woke up, I knew it was THE DAY!

A woman on a mission, I hurried to the store to buy the apples and other ingredients and items required to make lots of little jars of apple butter. These would then be distributed at Christmas or whenever anyone came to the house for a visit.

Coming back, I got everything well under way in my small kitchen. The huge pot filled with apples was boiling. Another pot was on another burner sterilizing the jars. And all was right with the world!

This was my special day. My day to do somethings that brought me so much pleasure. Therefore, it was not a day to be interrupted. I couldn't stop until I had filled and sealed the very last jar, which wouldn't be opened again until it was ready to grace someone's breakfast table for their hot biscuits or toast.

Happy as a clam, I was humming and singing and cooking when a loud slam of the door burst through my self-made music, and loud footsteps rushed into the kitchen. The pastor was home! And with his appearance in my kitchen came these words . . .

"Hurry! Get dressed. We have to be at the funeral home!"

I don't mean to sound cruel, but I'll admit that my apple butter was a bit more important to me as I inquired about this funeral. I hadn't heard that anyone at church had died, and certainly no one in our family had passed on to glory. So, I really didn't see the need for my attendance.

Every one of my kitchen-focused thoughts left my head like air out of a whale's blowhole, and I couldn't even think straight staring at the seriousness on my husband's face. As most women will tell you, if you want us to walk away from something we've set our minds on as seeming of the utmost importance, it had better be something monumental.

As this didn't seem to be one of those moments for me, I proceeded to stir the apple butter and drain the hot jars while he stood there. I was now ready to fill the jars with this delicious, sweet, melt-in-your-mouth delicacy when I realized something. He was really serious!

That had me calming down enough to ask appropriate questions, starting with, "Who died?"

His reply: "I don't know."

This wasn't going well. Yet our conversation continued.

"Think, honey! You must know who the deceased person is. How else will you be able to do the funeral?"

"If I knew, I'd tell you," he said. "The funeral home called, and they need a preacher for someone who doesn't have a preacher. I don't know anything about him, but I feel like I need to do this."

That was not sitting well with me.

He pressed on. "Now, please hurry and get dressed. This is a last-minute thing happening here, and I have to go. I need you with me! You know, the preacher's wife."

Let me tell you, I was not in the mood to go to the funeral of someone I didn't even know, especially on the spur-of-the-moment. I was in the middle of making apple butter! My mind and every bone in my body screamed that this was MY DAY! After all, the mood might not hit again for months. Maybe years! This apple butter had to be made. *Now!*

I felt like a gang of giants were dancing across my forehead and eyeballs, a sensation I did not appreciate. My anger was building—hardly a good quality for the "preacher's wife." I mean, bless the dear departed one's heart. They couldn't help it if it was my apple butter day and their time to go. But really!

It took all my composure to turn off the burners; lay aside my jars, dish towels, and utensils; and leave the apple butter in the pot. The gang of giants were still at it, running around my mind saying, *I'll get even. You can't mess up my apple butter day without consequences. Just you wait and see, bucko!*

Besides, I had begun to think of myself as "not your typical preacher's wife," and those words kept echoing in my head.

Hey, I try really hard; but sometimes, the flesh wins.

I imagine most preacher's wives would have gently stopped what they were doing, hugged their preacher husbands, offered to pray for the family of the deceased, and quietly and meekly gotten dressed. Not me though. I plotted.

Nobody messes up my apple butter day. Get dressed? Okay. I'll get dressed!

I hurried to the closet to decide what to wear, my imagination going wild.

Let's see. I can wear that really short skirt and a low-cut top, put on lots of make-up, chew some gum, and go parading into the funeral home late and looking like a floozie. I'll just march down to the casket and cry and cry.

His wife will think I was the mistress!

Thank heavens, my sense of decency kicked in, and I had to ask for forgiveness for even thinking such a thing. But I still felt like a bat with a radar malfunction. While I did the good pastor's wife thing, dressed modestly, and sat in the back row, I thought about my apple butter the whole time. Shame on me!

Patience, quite obviously, isn't my greatest virtue.

When we got back, the apple butter was completed and set on the shelf to await its new owners. All's well that ends well, but I prayed that nothing like that would ever happen again.

Little did I know of future experiences that would take place — at funerals!

❊

Other than that apple butter day, I'd make a wonderful mourner for anyone's funeral. That's because I'm such an easy crier. I can cry at library dedication services. How bad is that?

For all the obvious reasons, I don't know of anyone who likes to attend funerals. But there's also the fact that they serve as reminders for what the Bible tells us: that it's appointed unto man once to die. So we know that day is coming for us sometime in our own lives.

I like to think I'll pass away in my sleep, free from pain, still happily married to my "preacher man." However, things don't always work out the way we want them to, as well most of us know.

Many people prepare for their funeral as well as their futures. My mother, for one, was the editor for the local newspaper for more than 40 years. She loved to write and told me she already had all her service arrangements in writing and stored in her underwear drawer.

Sure enough, when the time came, I found it right where she said.

I've always assumed that, because she was a writer, she just loved to get all her thoughts on paper, no matter how long it took me to read. She passed away a few years ago, but would you believe I'm still finding little notes in all her personal belongings (not her underwear drawer). They remind me to be sure to contact this person or that person, complete with smiley faces drawn on each page.

The apple, I've found, doesn't fall far from the tree since I've since done the same thing. I've written all my arrangements and have them ready for whoever finds me and needs to make the necessary preparations. You probably won't be surprised that, as I was writing my own obituary and funeral plans, I got a bit carried away. Before I knew it, I was laughing myself into tears. What I wrote was just too funny!

Perhaps it will also make my loved ones smile someday, easing their pain when I step from this life into eternity. Isn't that what we all want for the people we leave behind for a little while longer?

While I believe that funerals ought to be reverent, I also think they should be relaxed and involve humor. In my particular case, I think someone will have a wonderful time with that task when my life is filled with so much humor already.

The Bible says laughter does us good like a medicine, and I believe it. When I was the church secretary and someone would call, perhaps feeling a bit down, I'd have them laughing before the conversation was over. They would always thank me, and tell me they felt so much better afterward—further proof that the Bible can be trusted. I read somewhere else that it's a proven fact that people who laugh a lot live longer.

Personally, I'm hoping for 125 years or more!

With that said, laughing during funerals has probably been a no-no throughout history, no doubt due to respecting the deceased's family. I understand this as a human being and as a preacher's wife, an occupation that's seen me attending my share of funerals. However, some just sort of stand out from others. Like the following . . .

One year, a very good friend of ours lost her husband to cancer. We loved them both dearly and were devastated when we heard he had this horrible disease. As time went on and he became weaker each day, we knew it wouldn't be long before he wouldn't be with us anymore. It was obvious to everyone, his wife included, though she managed to keep her sense of humor throughout the painful ordeal.

When the time came, my husband had the honor of officiating at his funeral. The deceased was an Army veteran and a proud American, and the funeral service was designed to portray that.

I'd never been to a funeral that was held at night before, but this one was in the evening at a nearby funeral home. A large crowd from our church family was there to pay their respects at the visitation and then at the funeral itself immediately after. It was a beautiful tribute, and all was going as well as could be expected as everyone made their way to the pews to be seated.

There was no reason for my preacher husband to not feel confident he could leave his find-humor-in-everything wife without supervision among the congregation.

It was a wonderful service, too. I was seated next to our dearest friends, but because she was prone to having to go to the bathroom so often, her husband decided to let her sit on the pew in the seat next to the aisle, putting him next to me. I was doing so well, behaving myself, listening intently to the message my husband had prepared for the family.

I maintain what happened next wasn't my fault.

None of us—not even the preacher—knew that, just outside the funeral home doors, there would be a military detail assigned to the service. Evidently, the funeral home director gave a signal; and before anyone knew what was happening, guns were being fired. Loud and clear. With the doors being left open for that very purpose, it was like they were right next to us.

My friend on the outside pew shot up in the air about six inches! Her husband, a big, strapping man next to me, was next in line to jump. Then me. Looking around, I could see all our church members resembling so many Mexican jumping beans popping up and down, eyes glazed, yet otherwise frozen with fear. Meanwhile, up at the altar, old preacher man (hubby) went into his Vietnam PTSD mode as if Rambo had taken over his body.

Personally, I lost count of the firing guns after the third one went off. That may have been because I went hysterical at the sight of all the Mexican jumping beans. I'm not sure, but I think a few folks behind me hit the floor and hid under the pews. Not that I can blame them. When I flew up into the air after gunshot number one, I came down so hard it was like playing Whack-a-Mole with my behind.

That wasn't the end of it either. Before we knew it, there were sirens blaring and blue lights flashing. Someone in the neighborhood heard the gunshots and called the police.

And my friend who sat on the outside pew so she could easily slip out to the bathroom? Well, she didn't need to go anymore. The gunfire took care of it for her. I'm honestly not sure how long it took the funeral home to dry those pews.

Our friend, the widow, still laughs about both the service and our reactions. Understandably so. It was very melodramatic. Yet it's also proof of how a sense of humor is so important in life, whether Christian or not. Sometimes, it eases painful and emotional stress just when we need it most.

At the time that particular laugh-fest took place, I genuinely believed it couldn't be topped. And maybe it can't be. But there was another funeral we attended that comes in close second in this regard.

Fortunately, my husband wasn't the officiating minister that time. But the deceased was the mother of a dear friend of ours, so we felt we needed to be there for her. We went with other good friends (the same ones I sat with at the other funeral, in fact), the service was very nice, and we headed to the cemetery for the burial afterward.

I had no idea where we were, only that we traveled somewhere through the woods to get there. Then, all of a sudden, we were at a cemetery.

Now, me being me, I included in my own witty funeral plans for a little artificial, feathered bluebird to be presented to each of my children and grandchildren so they could place them on my casket during the burial. Afterward, they could each take their bluebird home with them as a remembrance of their mom/grandma. I also seriously had someone lined up to sing "Somewhere Over the Rainbow" as they place said bluebirds on the casket.

A nice touch, I thought.

I've seen doves released at weddings before. That's always a tender, moving moment. But never at a funeral before. Yet, at this particular cemetery out in the woods, someone released doves or pigeons or whatever they were, which then flew into the sky. It was during this most serious moment that a crazy thought slipped into my mind. Without warning, I was imagining some old redneck, Bubba, seeing those birds flying off and Bam! Bam! Bam! He'd go home to his wife and say, "Honey, you'll never guess what I got you for supper tonight. There was a whole covey of 'em."

Worse yet, I could imagine what would happen to the family of the deceased at seeing all those dead birds falling to the ground.

Naturally, with the vision of doves dropping and guns blasting (again), I began to laugh. I just can't help myself sometimes.

Fortunately, in such situations, I've learned that if you get tickled, you can always put the Kleenex to your mouth, eyes, and nose, and people will think you're mourning the departed. Been there; done that. It works!

My husband did manage to find a bit of humor in the vision when I told him my crazy thoughts later, though not as much as I did.

Chapter 5

We Ain't Got No Frank!

Another time, we received a call from one of our church members that his brother, who lived in another town about an hour away, had passed. Naturally, he was saddened with the news and we certainly empathized with him. He told us he'd let us know when the funeral arrangements had been decided and were confirmed, and we assured him we would be in attendance. In fact, many of our church family members would want to be there, too.

To be respectful of the family, I won't use the deceased's last name, only his first, as this story continues.

The night of the visitation arrived and we hurriedly left work, rushed home to change clothes, and left once more in hopes of getting to the services on time. We knew where the little town was located, but not the funeral home. As we made our way into town, everything looked dark and abandoned. It felt like we drove for hours in that disturbing ambiance, but it was only for a few minutes.

When we didn't find the place, we turned around and headed in the opposite direction. Still no sighting though. Desperate, we stopped at a convenience store and my hubby went in to ask directions. Here's what they told him . . .

"Well, ya just drive down the road for a ways — not a long ways — and ya cain't miss it."

These were the directions from someone wearing a Sheriff's uniform, by the way. Not sure if it was a real uniform or if they were going to a costume party. He didn't look like someone with a lot of authority though, a fact that didn't make me feel any better considering the area and the not-so-welcome looks I was receiving from other inhabitants.

Hubby got back in the car where I was sitting, frightened out of my skin, and relayed the information. Then off we went again into the unknown. As instructed, we drove down the road "for a ways, not a long ways" but still didn't see a funeral home. What we did see was a motel — the kind of establishment I'm sure I wouldn't ever want to spend a night in. But hubby dutifully went inside while I stayed put, hoping no one would see him enter. Wouldn't it be just like some of our church members to pass by on the way to the funeral home, wherever in the world it was located, and see the preacher going into Sleaze Motel!

To my knowledge, that didn't happen. Thank goodness.

He got back to the car unscathed with new directions, which meant we were turning around again to go back to the same area we landed the first time. By then, we were beginning to think it was all a prank, that the brother hadn't really died, that the visitation was a figment of someone's overactive imagination, and that there certainly wasn't any funeral home. But it was at that point that I, the preacher's wife, did the bright thing and called information. The operator who answered went on to immediately and without my permission connect me.

I'm going to do my best to relay the conversation we had while my husband kept driving.

"H-e-l-l-o!" a man shouted into my ear.

I thought this couldn't possibly be the place—not by the way he answered the phone—so I meekly squeaked out, "Is this the funeral home?"

"Yeah. Sure is!"

Maybe he thought I was hard of hearing and that's why he was shouting, but I still continued in my soft, trying-to-sound-confident voice. Do you have a Frank there?

"Hold on!"

I waited and waited for him to return to the phone, hoping for a helpful answer.

That hope was in vain. "Who didya say?"

"Frank."

"Hold on," said the funeral home director/visitor/janitor/whoever I was speaking with.

I had no idea. He was very unprofessional though, and if we hadn't been in such a hurry, it would have been humorous. Admittedly, it wouldn't be too long before we found the humor in all of it and laughed ourselves silly. But that was a few more minutes down the road.

He came back to the phone, still shouting. "Who is 'dis?"

I really didn't think it was necessary to give my name, so I just politely replied, "I'm trying to locate a Frank who should be in your funeral home."

His reply: "Hold on!"

I was almost sure at that point that if the services were genuine the visitation must be over, the funeral was done, the body had been buried, and everyone had gone home. I was trying desperately to keep it together, but I was beginning to feel those inner giggle bubbles start to come to life.

Finally, after another several minutes, the man came back to the phone. "We ain't got no Frank! We's got a Krayshon!"

As mentioned before, I'm just using first names to protect the innocent, but the "Frank" I was trying to find and the "Krayshon" he had found did have the same last name. It made me wonder if that could be Frank's middle name. But it just didn't quite fit, so I thanked him kindly and asked if there happened to be another funeral home in the area.

His shout was clear. Very clear. "Yeah! Dere's one over across town! But they ain't no need to go dere! They ain't got no bodies over dere!"

Well now, what did we do? As a last resort, I called our friend, the brother of the deceased, and explained that we didn't have a clue where we were. And was his brother's middle name Krayshon?

He burst out laughing, and then I started howling with laughter, too. After we'd calmed down some, he gave directions to the actual building that held Frank's beloved body, saying he would stand in the street and wave when he saw us. We did eventually spot him in the street, flapping his arms and still laughing. I guess it sort of helped ease the tension and sadness for him when I relayed why I was wondering about his brother's middle name, because every time we tried to walk inside the funeral home after that, we became hysterical with laughter. There we stood like three crazy loons, laughing uncontrollably.

That third person laughing was my preacher boy, who tries so hard to maintain some sort of dignity and composure to make up for his wife's craziness.

Nor was the craziness over quite yet. While in the funeral home paying our respects to the family, in walked one of our deacons who happens to be a very close friend to the brother (who happened to still be laughing). None of us outsiders knew that the deceased was a spitting image of his brother, our friend. They weren't twins, but they could have easily passed as such. So when our deacon walked in and looked at the body in the casket, he yelped, grabbed his heart, started turning in circles, and saying, "Oh, my Lord! Oh, my Lord!"

I became hysterical all over again, as did the living brother. And when the deacon friend realized what had happened, he began to laugh right along with the rest of us. It got so bad that I was truly afraid the funeral home director — who was much more professional than his counterpart across town — was going to ask us to please vacate the building and never come back.

All's well that ends well, I suppose.

But then there are those days when you think everything is going well and there have been no emergencies or mishaps, only for something to come up that changes the whole day. That's how I felt when our own local funeral home called again saying it needed a pastor to conduct a funeral. And, again, this story requires a few background details. Specifically about the car we owned at the time.

It was a Mercury Marquis, and it had been a very reliable car for a very long time, always comfortable and meeting our vehicular needs. There was a problem, however. As the car aged, the seats were becoming too soft and too sunken in, which is a huge problem for me since I'm rather short in stature. Because of this, I finally had to start relying on not one but two pillows to hoist me up to see over the dashboard and out the window.

In addition, every time someone got into the car, the springs would make this horrible squeaking sound. And not only had the seats taken a lot of wear and tear through the years, but one of the hubcaps on the driver's side had come off, too, and rolled into some ditch where it would never be found. Not by us, anyway. A few days later, another hubcap on the passenger's side followed suit, also never to be reclaimed.

Hubby's intentions were to replace them as soon as he had some free time. But again, this was a last-minute call. So we didn't have time to get that done, much less wash the car, which he always liked to do for a funeral.

Now, at a funeral, protocol says that the officiating pastor is to lead the way in front of the hearse. So there we went, driving to the funeral with a missing hubcap on each side of the dirty car, and me sitting on two pillows. It struck me as funny (not surprising, I know) that we must look like two old Southern rednecks between the already-listed factors and the bird poop all over the vehicle. (Also not surprisingly), that had me laughing and giggling all the way through the service.

When it ended, I took hubby's hand on the way out of the funeral home, inspired with a brilliant idea. "I was thinking during the service, why can't we take off the hubcap on the driver's side and slap it on the passenger's side? Then it will look like we have a full set of hubcaps!"

That side was, after all, facing the people and the funeral home.

His response was much more logical. "And what do we do when we get to the cemetery, and the other side of the car with no hubcaps is facing the people?"

Oh, my goodness, it just sounded so funny when he put it that way that I began to do my belly-roll laughter. And I couldn't stop. I was in such bad shape that I had to jerk the two pillows out from under me, throw them in the backseat, and sink down to below dash-level, where I laughed until I cried.

Needless to say, at the cemetery, I sat in the car while hubby got out of his soon-to-be-traded-in car and proceeded with his pastoral duties.

Chapter 6

A Serious Side?

It takes a great amount of faith to do the things God asks you to do—to follow Him wherever He leads. As you can imagine, faith is a huge part of my Christian life, and it's sustained me in so many situations that would have otherwise been disastrous.

This includes being a preacher's wife, which, as I've found, takes a tremendous amount of trust. For one, I have faith in my husband to always be faithful to me, to be my friend and companion for life, to trust me, and to share his thoughts and feelings with me as I do with him.

Does that sound like marriage in general? Well, yes. And, at the same time, no.

Preachers' wives must trust their husbands when they have to make late night calls to the hospital, or to the home of someone on the verge of suicide, or to get involved in a domestic family problem. They need to trust God, too, whenever they start feeling that the church and its people come first, asking for strength to still believe in their husband's calling, pray for them, and be there for them at all times.

As for me, when occasions came up where I had to give up my time with my spouse, or when our already-made plans had to change because of a church need, I always tried hard to find some humor in it (except when it came to apple butter). That isn't always easy, but I've found that laughter — or at least smiling — makes the situation seem less monumental. And sometimes, it comes quite naturally, like the time one of our really great friends had a family member in the hospital.

My husband had gotten home from a long and full day at work where he'd counseled, visited the sick, studied for his sermon, and made several phone calls. Understandably, he was tired. Yet, just after he'd finished his evening meal, changed into his pajamas, and sat down to rest in his recliner, the phone rang.

I was sitting on the sofa when he picked it up and said hello, so I noticed the change in his expression right away. It seemed that a whispered female voice had asked, "What are you wearing?"

Perhaps if he'd been rested enough mentally, he could have answered like the TV commercial with "khakis." However, he wasn't sure who was calling because of the low voice and volume. So, he went with the more accurate "pajamas" instead.

The next thing I knew, he was smiling, making me really begin to wonder what in the world was going on right there in front of me. My curiosity rose further when he spoke her name and started to laugh.

As it turned out, this friend of ours was in the hospital room with a family member. She was whispering so as not to disturb the doctor, who had just walked in, and she wanted to know her preacher's attire because she knew it was late and didn't want to ask him to come to the hospital if he was all ready for bed. This dear, sweet woman simply didn't word that concern quite as well as she could have.

We laughed ourselves silly about that one. And then my husband graciously changed his clothes and went to go out again. But it's been a running joke among the three of us ever since, with our conversations usually beginning with, "What are you wearing?"

With all these funny moments to share, you might be doubting my previous claim that sometimes it's hard to smile, much less laugh. You're probably wondering if I ever get serious, but the answer is yes. I really do have a serious side to me, and I'll be the first person to offer to pray for you, sit with you, cry with you, or just listen to you if that's what you need. I'm a firm believer in prayer and the faithfulness of God; and, contrary to what you've read so far, I am able to put aside my crazy antics to be the friend you need.

I have a Ph.D. in Christian counseling, a degree I've practiced for many years. My husband, incidentally, has this same degree. So, we work together, meaning that I know firsthand and secondhand what a serious side the profession requires, complete with a lot of faith and trust. But humor can be useful as well depending on the situation, making it easier for people to relax and open up.

So many might think I'm not the typical preacher's wife, and maybe I'm not. But God gave me a sense of humor, and I firmly believe he wants me to use it when it applies.

I know I already mentioned becoming the music director of our church. As such, I was always looking for new choir members and new music to play. This was something I definitely took seriously as I tried to bring music into our worship services that honored God and was joyful to sing.

Slowly but surely, the choir began to grow, too. It was wonderful to watch! And one of the members in particular was an absolute delight. A prissy little bit in her eighties at the time, she probably weighed less than 95 pounds, dressed like a little teenager, and didn't care if anyone looked scornfully at her. She was her own person with personality-plus, and everyone loved her.

She also promised to hand down her clothes to me when she passed despite how I hadn't seen 95 pounds in 60 years or more. But she thought it was so neat that I'd inquired about her apparel. Really, I was joking with her about it because I knew it made her feel younger; I'd look like a stuffed sausage in some of her clothes — a would-be teenaged stuffed sausage.

One day, she told me that she might be out of the choir for a while because she was having her teeth pulled and would be getting new dentures. When she returned, now fitted with her new dentures, she was excited to show off her new teeth, smiling a big Colgate smile and all. But she still pulled me to the side to confess, "I'm not sure if they'll stay in my mouth. They feel funny."

I assured her they'd be fine. She just had to get used to them.

On Sunday morning as the choir assembled in the choir room, we practiced our special song one last time before going into the sanctuary. Everything sounded like it was going to run smoothly. And, sure enough, everything went along smoothly until the choir stood up to sing their special.

I smiled at my friend with the new teeth, and she smiled back. But I couldn't help but notice how she didn't give the same big smile she had earlier. No problem. I figured she must be a little self-conscious. Even the boldest of us get that way sometimes. So, we began to sing as planned, the choir belting out their beautiful harmony on cue.

Now, this dear lady was in the front row directly in front of me. That placed me perfectly to see her open her mouth wide for one particular note. Without further ado, out flew her teeth.

She was grabbing thin air trying to reclaim them, and I was reaching out with one hand to grab them for her while directing with the other. It was quite the sight to see from my angle!

Fortunately, she managed to catch them before they hit the floor, and she was able to cram them back into her mouth. Also fortunately, because she was directly in front of me, very few folks in the congregation saw what happened. Nor did most of the choir.

Everyone kept singing.

I kept directing.

And she quickly made the necessary readjustment.

But by that point, I was so tickled and laughing so hard, I could hardly see the music.

The choir saw me laughing and began to grin as well even though they had no idea what had happened. In short, we looked like the happiest choir in the county. Praise the Lord!

One church hat I didn't have to wear was activities director. We had a very competent woman in charge of that, and she would often plan trips for anyone who wanted to go. Our best trips, in my opinion, were the ones we took to Amish country in Lancaster, Pennsylvania. We would drive a caravan of cars, and in our particular one, we had the same people go with us each time. There was so much laughter and fun during that long drive that it never seemed very long.

While in Lancaster, this wonderful activities director of ours had planned for us to go to the live drama, "Jonah," at Sight & Sound Theaters. We were all excited about the play because we'd heard so many wonderful things about the actors' professionalism and the stage's elaborate beauty and special effects.

Sure enough, it was impressive. The story of Jonah and the whale itself might be familiar, but we'd never seen it portrayed in such a lifelike manner before.

With the music swelling and the actors projecting, the tale took off, showing one scene after another until the part where Jonah was to be swallowed up. Lights were already dim by then, helping to hide the long sticks various stagehands were using to hold the fish high up in the air as it "swam" past our rows of seats. It was as if we were in the water with the fish, and everyone was mesmerized by the majestic likeness as it floated over our heads.

However, as it tends to do, my brain managed to come up with something funny right at that inspiring moment. As I looked up and saw the long sticks attached to the huge fish, I couldn't help it. I thought I was saying it quietly, but I guess that wasn't the case when everything else in that huge room was so quiet already. So my voice echoed a bit louder than planned.

All I said was, "Look. Fish on a stick. Fish sticks." It really wasn't all that funny, but perhaps it was the way I said it. Our row of people tried so hard to be quiet, and most of them succeeded. But when I heard others snickering, I doubled over in laughter. I didn't mean for a large portion of the strangers sitting on other rows to start laughing, but they did.

This left my husband, Preacher Boy, to just look down and shake his head. He's learned by now that he must accept me for who I am.

I'm not sure if it was on that same trip to Amish country or another one, but everyone in our group decided we needed ice cream. We were all dressed up and looking very nice, but one of the ladies who rode with us is particularly immaculate in her wardrobe, with matching shoes, purses, and jewelry. My dream one day is to go to her house and stand and gaze at her jewelry collection and her closet of beautiful clothes. That's how nice she always looks.

Anyway, we were at the ice cream shop and had ordered our sundaes, when she needed to use the restroom. She gracefully paraded herself the rather long walk there, and all eyes were on her, I'm sure admiring her attire. Every hair was in place. Her makeup was flawless. Her attire was exquisite. None of those details had changed when she returned, though there was one added to the mix—a very long piece of toilet paper stuck to her beautiful high heel shoe.

I've heard stories of this happening or where a skirt is tucked up in panty hose, but I'd never seen it until that night. It struck me as just so funny, and—surprise, surprise, I know—I began to laugh. When she arrived at the table, I couldn't even get the words out to tell her about her unintentional accessory no matter how hard I tried. I had to give up and point.

She was so embarrassed, though not enough that she couldn't laugh as well. Moreover, what did she do? If it had been me, I would have tried to step on it with the other foot or scraped it on the floor as inconspicuously as possible. But nope! Not her. She held her head high, pulled back those shoulders and elegantly made the long walk back to the bathroom, toilet paper trailing right behind her.

I couldn't even eat my ice cream for laughing. By that time, the entire table of folks were hysterical, with even Preacher Boy having to wipe his eyes from laughter.

Speaking of my dear hubby, he does have a sense of humor even if it's nothing at all like mine. Sometimes, he can come up with some dry humor that not only surprises me but makes me laugh.

That was the case on another of those trips to Amish country. The group had been to one of the largest buffets I've ever seen, and we were all feeling completely stuffed. As we started driving back to the motel, the same two ladies who were always our "car buddies" were in the backseat. We were chatting and laughing as usual when we came upon an accident. It wasn't anything critical, but I think it involved one of the Amish buggies that were so prevalent around the area. An ambulance was already there and everything was under control, so we drove on.

About three or four minutes down the road, we saw an Amish boy on a scooter with a tiny whizzing motor that sounded like a swarm of bumblebee wings as it slowly passed us by. All my husband dryly said was, "Amish Rescue Squad," and the three of us ladies completely lost it. It hasn't proved funny to anyone else except the four of us, but the way he said it, the timing, and the larger situation was more than we could take.

Admittedly, that made the rest of the ride rather uncomfortable. Three menopausal ladies with full bladders wasn't a pretty sight for Preacher Boy.

And then one last story about Amish Country. There the four of us were another time, riding and laughing and talking and snacking. It was a "free day," which meant we all got to go off in different directions. But many of us had decided to tour the Amish village. At the time, I was having some difficulty with my vision because I needed new glasses but hadn't taken time to get them yet. That meant I had to ask more than once, "What does that sign say?" or "What is that in front of that store?"

We were walking along, enjoying everything, when we came across one such moment. That's when I spotted a horse standing in the middle of the walkway a short distance from us, prompting me to ask why anyone would leave a horse just standing in the middle of a walkway. Everyone started laughing, but I didn't know what was so funny until we got a little closer and saw it was a cow, not a horse.

Okay. Fine. But why would they have a cow in the middle of the walkway? Stepping even closer, I finally noticed it wasn't a real cow, just a model of one. I'm not sure, but I think it was one of those things where you could have your picture taken. Under normal circumstances, I don't know why anyone would want to. But considering my silly mistake, guess who had to do exactly that?

Not only did I pose for a picture, but I noticed that the cow had all its parts. So, naturally, I reached down to pretend to milk it. Yet as I pulled on its teats, the whole udder fell off into my hands. I didn't know what to do holding that horrible-looking thing in my hands, so I laughed! And then I laughed some more while I desperately tried to fit it back on, lining up the hinges and screws — to no avail.

People passing by started laughing and taking pictures of me, the preacher's wife with cow udders in hand. I posed for them, so some of you may have seen such images on Facebook. Though I truly hope not!

About the only thing my husband said about all that was, "We have GOT to get you some new glasses."

Chapter 7

Gone With the Wind

We hadn't been at our church very long before I decided, as the music director, to inquire about having a spaghetti dinner fund raiser to help purchase some things for our music department. With everyone in favor of it, I began to make plans.

At that time, we had a very small area in our fellowship hall/educational building. The kitchen was tiny, and there was an adjoining room where all the food would be placed. Really, there was hardly room to turn around back there, so when the kitchen workers were cooking or serving food, it was almost impossible to move without running into each other. Even so, we worked out a plan so serving the spaghetti wouldn't be such a hassle.

We began doling it out around noon with the goal of staying open until seven. And it stayed fairly busy, though there were lulls in the action which gave all the kitchen workers a short time to rest. Seated in the tiny "food room" was one of our volunteer servers who had a great Texas drawl. It was even more pronounced than the ones we North Carolinians sported. He was leaning his chair against the wall, waiting until the next group arrived when in walks another one of our church members.

This gentleman was tall, slender, and had a wonderful personality; but he was new and didn't know too many of our folks yet. He did, however, know the Texan, who I'll keep calling that for anonymity's sake. New Member, I'll call "B."

I'm not sure if "B" was having some intestinal gas problems because of something he ate or if there was a medical issue. But there was something going on as he stood tall talking to Texan. Despite how small the room was, he didn't notice me walk into the little room with a plate of spaghetti, which happens all the time. I'm short in stature (what I call "fun size") and easy to overlook. So "B" had no idea I was right behind him trying to squeeze through the small space.

Of course, that's when it happened. The gas problem was solved.

Now, being short, I was right there, nose to rear. And folks, I've never heard such a sound. There is no bullhorn that could possibly compare.

I stood there, petrified, horrified, and gagging. But since "B" was a new member, I didn't want him to be embarrassed. I had every intention of backing up until I was in the kitchen, leaving him clueless about what had happened. Yet I found myself unable to move, feeling as if my hair had been parted or singed, and I was most definitely going to be throwing out my plate of spaghetti.

There are no secrets with Texan. He saw me standing there with who-knows-what-kind-of-expression on my face and spaghetti in hand. Still laid back against the wall in his chair, he nonchalantly said in his Southern drawl, "We-l-l-l, for goodness sake. I cain't believe ya just did that, and you did it on the preacher's wife!"

"B" turned around quickly, and boy, was his face red—beet red. He kept apologizing, but all I could do was laugh. I guess my laughter broke the ice, and soon he was laughing, too. Like such stories should, it became a joke between the three of us; and every once in a while, the story comes up and we laugh all over again.

In "B"'s defense, I've been nicknamed "The Toot Magnet." It seems those things find me no matter where I am. And yes, it's happened more times than I care to count. Being short isn't always what it's "cracked" up to be. Sometimes I feel like I'm in a cloud — and it isn't pleasant.

�֎

One of my most favorite books to ever be made into a movie is *Gone With the Wind*. It's one of those stories you can read over and over, or watch numerous times. If you've ever seen it yourself, you might recall a little slave girl named Prissy. In which case, you'll probably remember that scene where Scarlett O'Hara's sister is going to give birth, and Scarlett is frantically trying to get help. Finding Prissy, she tells her to go act as midwife, but Prissy makes the tearful pronouncement to Scarlett in a shrill voice, "No, Miss Scarlett, I don't know nothin' 'bout birthin' no babies!"

Please keep that phrase in mind as I tell you about another of my experiences.

It happened in the summer when there was to be a funeral service at the church cemetery. We had a limited amount of space in the small cemetery, and it was almost full except for one last family plot. The deceased lived out of town but always wanted to be buried in the church cemetery.

I didn't know the family, but they were going to have the service at the graveside with their own pastor from out of town officiating. But I was working in my church office on the other side of the sanctuary while mourners arrived in their cars.

As I sat at my desk and watched the cars fill the parking lot, one particular man stood out. He didn't look like he was there for a funeral since he was wearing shorts and sandals. His long gray hair hung around his shoulders, and his expression told me that trouble might be brewing. Sure enough, as I'd already expected, he didn't walk across the yard to go past the sanctuary to the cemetery.

My husband wasn't there at the time. He was off doing some "preacher thing," so I was at the office alone. Recognizing how isolated I was, I began to feel uneasy but tried to keep calm. It didn't help much when I realized I'd forgotten to lock the glass storm door.

My nervous system was humming with one word on repeat: "Dummy. Dummy. Dummy!"

He opened the door, walked in, and stood in front of me.

Prayer time! I was praying so hard in my mind! You have no idea.

As for him, he didn't say hello or give any kind of greeting. He just stared at me. And the first words out of his mouth were, "Where'd ya put them dead bodies?"

You know how people who are faced with impending death will say they saw their lives flash before their eyes? Not me! I didn't see anything flashing before me except the very real possibility that, if I should meet the Lord that day, my husband would find me and not know what in the world had happened.

I knew for sure I was going to have a heart attack.

With my mouth feeling like it was stuffed with cotton balls filled with peanut butter, I managed to squeak out, "Excuse me?"

He repeated his question. "Them dead bodies. Where'd ya put 'em?"

This is where I could have been featured in *Gone With the Wind* as I squeaked out again, this time in a voice pitched higher than Prissy's, "I don't know nothin' 'bout no dead bodies!"

This was getting really weird, and I was getting really frightened as he proceeded to tell me that our Family Life Center was built over a graveyard. I assured him it wasn't, but he went on and on about the dead bodies, wanting to know where we put them when we dug up the ground.

What do you do with someone like that?

Finally, he switched subjects. "That's my mama over there that's going to be buried today."

Seizing on that very odd lifeline, I did my best to sound calm. "Don't you think you need to go to the cemetery? I'm sure the service has started, and I know your mama would want you there."

He stared at me. Then gave a single, "Yeah," turned, and walked out the door.

With knocking knees and perspiration on my body, I managed to get to the storm door. I locked that thing; shut the main door; locked it, too; turned out the lights; and collapsed in my chair. This was not a belly-laughing event!

That is until I began to relay it to my husband and friends. That's when it all began to sound so funny. What a ridiculous scenario, indeed!

Every once in a while now, someone will just ask that one question, "What'd ya do with them dead bodies?" and we'll laugh ourselves silly.

Chapter 8

Now, Don't You Feel Better?

A long with the aging process comes new aches and pains, making us wonder how in the world one body can have so many different parts. I'm no different from any other person my age, so I'm not surprised when I wake up each morning with the Rice Krispie syndrome . . .

Snap. Crackle. Pop!

As it so happened one morning, I awoke and felt a twinge in my lower back. And while I tried to go about my workday as usual, I just kept wiggling and squirming like a worm in hot ashes. When it just wouldn't get any better, I thought I'd go to a chiropractor to see if he could yank out the kink.

Now, you have to understand this about me. Other than my yearly checkup, I don't go to doctors unless I absolutely have to. But on this day, I was in great need of relief, so I gave in. Having no idea which chiropractor to choose, I finally decided on one whose first name was David.

It sounded biblical, so he couldn't be all bad.

Women especially, you'll understand this part: how, when you go to the doctor, you usually wear your nicer underclothes just in case you have to sit there in a gown that won't fit because it's way too small instead of the gown that would fit Goliath the Giant that forces you to wrap it around yourself six times. Sometimes, they give you a tiny wash cloth to cover your body, which means your nice underwear comes in handy.

That day was no different for me. I didn't know if going to the chiropractor would be the same routine as my own family doctor, hence the reason I wore my best undies—just in case I had to put on a gown or part of a gown.

Upon arriving at the fateful location, hubby at my side, I told him to wait for me in the waiting area. After all, I'd be back soon—at least, that's what I hoped when they put me in a room and directed me to sit in a chair and relax.

I did.

Then a nice young girl who looked to be about 12 years old informed me how she'd be attaching a strip to my back. Apparently, it would pulsate in the painful area and I would feel lots of heat. She proceeded to attach a heavy, fake leather vest on top of my chest and shoulders that left me wondering if it was a bullet-proof vest. In which case, I'd better brace myself for the ride of a lifetime.

As it turned out, that last part was accurate. All of a sudden, it was like a porcupine had slipped between my back and the chair, and a zillion needles were tingling against my lower back.

I yelped, but she kept turning up the strength while using medical terms I didn't understand. It made me ask if she was speaking Swahili. What I did gather was her repeated question of, "Let me know if it's too much or if I can continue to turn up the strength."

By that time, my teeth were rattling, my eyes bulging, and the bullet-proof vest was getting heavier and heavier by the second. I could hardly breathe! I knew I was saved and going to heaven one day, but this felt like all the heat from the underworld was all over my body. All I could do was to hold up one finger while giving her a desperate "help me!" look.

She got that message at least, turning the machine off to ask, "Now, don't you feel better?"

If I'd been able to muster the strength, I probably would have had her neck in my tight hands. But being the preacher's wife, I just smiled and tried to nod.

I was sure my next stop would be a non-torture chamber where I could take off my sweat-drenched clothes and put on a gown. But not so! She led me to another area, where I managed to wobble on shaky legs to the table, walking like I had concrete blocks tied to my feet. When she told me to stretch out, I flopped down, not knowing what was coming next.

As she went on to inform me, it would be little rollers that would roll up and down my spine to begin to relax the tense muscles.

Considering her last description and the actual reality that followed, I braced myself for the expectation that they were going to roller skate up and down my back. Closing my eyes, I was seriously beginning to rethink this whole chiropractor thing well before the low rumbling began and a "little roller" bar came barreling onto my back to run all the way from my neck to the very end of my spine.

"This thing hurts!" I yelled.

But no one was in there. Opening my eyes, I noticed the lights had been turned off and there was only a dim light coming into the room from the hallway. Everyone had scattered like roaches at the end of a flashlight beam. And that rolling bar was already starting back up my back to travel its merry way to my neck.

"Oh, shoot!" I thought. "It's not only going down. Now it's going up, too!"

As quickly as the thought rushed into my mind, it started all over again. I'm not sure if I was conscious, but I think I kept yelling for help and thinking of that old familiar phrase: "What goes up must come down." Because that wretched rolling bar kept going up and down, and up and down.

After what seemed an eternity, the same little girl returned, flipped on the lights and said, "Betcha really feel better now, don't you?"

Oh, you have no idea the strength and fortitude it took to stay calm. You see, the preacher's wife couldn't lose control.

That wouldn't do. Though, speaking of the preacher, I could hear him in the waiting room talking and laughing with someone, completely clueless that his loving wife had been tortured within an inch of her life.

Had been tortured though. It was over. I could go home now, right? I didn't care if I ever actually saw the doctor. *Just get me out of here!*

But not so fast. Instead of showing me to the waiting room again, she guided my almost lifeless body into a tiny room and told me to sit in a chair.

What? No gown? That was probably a good thing. I don't think I could have gotten out of my clothes at that point anyway. Besides, the room felt like a tiny shoebox and colder than the mystery meat in the back of my freezer.

When the doctor finally came in, he shook my limp hand and introduced himself. I didn't care if he was King Kong; I just wanted out of that place.

I suppose I didn't clearly convey that to him because, after a few minutes of getting my life history, he told me he needed to get X-rays of my back. I was reluctant, of course. But by then, I just thought, *Why not. Let's just make it a day!* So I went through the X-rays and waited in the tiny arctic shoebox for him to return with the results.

When he finally came back, he immediately put the slides on the screen, letting me gaze at the strange-looking blackish-grayish outline. I recognized my ribs and some other parts, but there was one thing that really puzzled me: these little bubble-like circles up and down an area close to my spine. I'd never seen anything like them before in any of my high school or college science books, and I waited for him to declare me one in 10 zillion people to have some freakish condition.

Frightened almost beyond words, I managed to inquire about that detail, only to hear the most relieving diagnosis. They were gas bubbles! He said everyone has them, and that I was looking at my colon.

The fact that everyone has these cute little bubbles going up and down, and up and down their colon made me feel much better. Until he told me to stretch out on the cold slab of a table they'd managed to squeeze into the tiny arctic shoebox.

My inner voice whimpered. *No. Not another table.* Yet up I went anyway.

I've never been athletic, and I'm not familiar with the grueling exercises players go through to prepare their bodies for game times. But on this day, I found out firsthand what it must feel like.

He began to push and pull my body in all sorts of directions, wad me up in a ball, and roll me from side to side. When my legs came up under my chin, I pictured the X-ray film with all those gas bubbles, at which point this old preacher's wife began to pray. It went something like this...

"Oh, please, dear Jesus! Please, please, please don't let those gas bubbles escape. Help me, Lord. Please, please, please keep 'em in, Lord!"

Just one more push, pull, wad-in-a-ball, and knees-under-the-chin maneuver, and I knew I'd embarrass myself and the doctor, filling the tiny shoebox we were in with tiny bubbles, sort of like *The Lawrence Welk Show*. But instead, God answered my prayer, allowing me to finish dying with no such explosion. Upon which point, the doctor helped me off the table and told me to come back the next week so he could see what progress had been made, especially since I was to continue doing those "exercises."

He was out of his mind if he thought I was going to put myself through all that again, even at home! Yet, after talking to me a little longer, he somehow, someway managed to convince me that I needed to come back.

Maybe I had a slight touch of Stockholm's syndrome after all that torture? Maybe I was delirious from all the exertion. I don't know.

Out into the waiting room, I went where Preacher Boy sat and grabbed him by the hand to jerk him up out of his chair. "Let's go!"

It wasn't until we were in the car that I shared any of my experience. "Did you know you have gas bubbles in your colon?"

He looked at me as if I'd lost my mind and slowly said, "I guess so. Doesn't everybody?"

I could have knocked him into the next county.

The next week arrived, and it was time to go to the chiropractor again. Remembering that I didn't have to put on a gown the last time, I didn't bother to wear my very best underwear. In fact, I figured my old, everyday bra would suffice. After all, no one was going to see it, so why not be comfortable? All he was going to do was talk with me and maybe ask if I'd been doing those exercises for my back. Since my back felt a little better, I just assumed I wouldn't be put through the meat grinder again.

Never assume. Never.

This time, a different person called my name but led me right back to that same torture chamber I was in the first time. My eyes widened as I looked around the room. How could I have been so wrong?

Now, this other person wasn't as nice as the little girl I'd had the prior week. She was a bit on the rough side, with breath that could shrivel up a string of garlic. Though, even if that hadn't been the case, I would have known I was in trouble the second she pointed to that infamous chair.

Shaking with fear and trepidation, I sat down and once again began to call upon the Lord while the vest was slapped onto my chest and shoulders. Again, the strip was taped onto my back. Again, off I went into pain-filled oblivion. If this had been a POW situation, I probably would have told every military secret and divulged every plan I knew.

This thing was painful!

Being gracious the way He is, however, God not only didn't give me any such intelligence to divulge, but He also got me through the experience in one piece. Old Dragon Breath removed the items from my now tingling and sweaty body, and pointed to the next death chamber: the rolling table.

No! My brain started sobbing. *Not again! I thought I was just going to talk to the doctor! That's why I wore my old bra!*

After the roller blades had marred my back once more, I crawled off the table, found the tiny shoebox, and entered it, feeling as if I was at death's door all over again. The doctor entered, feeling much more chipper — and, no doubt, untortured — than I was. He gave his same friendly greeting and sat down to talk to me. Upon answering all his questions, I thought we were through. Until he told me to lie down on the table so he could check the condition of my back.

At least there was no gown. I was a happy camper about that aspect, remembering the gas bubbles of yester-week.

So, I got on the table, stretched out, and waited — only to be put through the same ordeal of being pulled, pushed, rolled in a ball, with knees tucked under my chin. Throughout this, I was still a little concerned about the colon bubbles but felt rather certain they were all in their perfect little places and not going to cause a scene.

What I didn't know was that he was going to take my arms, yank them high above my head, and pull and pull until I either broke in two or just died right there.

Remember the old bra I wore that day? Ladies know how stretched those things can get after so many washings and wearings, and mine was no exception. It was comfortable, yes, but not very tight-fitting: sort of reminded me of a good old pair of pajamas that have outlived anything else in the closet, and you know you should throw them away but can't because "they just feel so good."

Well, one arm went flying up thanks to the chiropractor's ministrations. And so did one cup of the bra.

Then the other arm went flying up. And so did the other cup of the bra.

So, there I was, stretched out on the table with the good doctor standing behind my head, pulling my arms with all his might. I felt it and, although I couldn't see it because I was in a stranglehold, there I knew sat my old, dilapidated, comfortable, washed-and-worn bra all up around my neck. I couldn't reach for it and pull it down, one cup at a time or otherwise, because my arms were stretched out to the waiting room—where my doubtlessly clueless preacher hubby once again sat and waited.

What could I do?

Ladies, have you ever tried to regroup those things and put them back in place at record speed while hoping the doctor doesn't see you? I couldn't have it so easy. Evidently, he spotted the "necklace" around my now red-as-a-beet neck, because he turned his back to me and began writing something at his desk. It was probably a note to tell his wife and entire staff about my predicament.

I was so embarrassed. I think I could have handled the gas bubbles better than what had actually happened. All I could see in my mind's eye was my body on the table and two pathetic "twinkies" pointing down, sideways, up, or wherever.

After I got myself situated, the doctor gave me a minute or two to compose myself, told me I was fine and that, if I had any problems, to please come back.

Not on your life, buddy!

Smiling as best I could, I thanked him, grabbed my purse, and then grabbed Preacher Boy by the hand with a four-word command. "Let's go. Right now!"

I never went back.

I even contemplated moving to another country.

Chapter 9

A Definite First

Oh, how can I ever forget my husband's first baptismal service?

Put simply, I can't.

We hadn't been at the church very long before new members were coming and joining our fellowship. One of them in particular wanted to be baptized, and this thrilled Preacher Boy! Upon examining the baptistery for the upcoming blessed event, he found it needed a super-cleaning, so he began to sweep it out and gather up the trash, even crawling underneath some part of the sanctuary to turn on the water. There was just one more pre-baptism detail that needed to be addressed.

Realizing that he didn't have any waders to wear, he called his best friend who was pastoring another church in the area. After discussing the matter, his friend told him he had a pair that he no longer used because their new sanctuary was designed just-so, and he didn't have to go into the water. Happy to help, he would get his old waders out of his attic and bring them over before Sunday.

The day arrived, and I was playing quiet music on the organ, preparing the atmosphere for the baptismal service while Hubby went upstairs to dress for the event. He had removed his suit coat, of course, but because he was wearing the waders, he didn't need to remove any of his other clothes except his shoes. So there he came back down, dressed in his Sunday shirt, tie, pants, socks, white baptismal robe, and borrowed waders, which, of course, couldn't be seen.

The actual baptism occurred without incident, but I noticed that he climbed out of the baptistery in what seemed like very slow motion. With no idea what was wrong, I kept the music going as the service continued and he got dressed to come back into the sanctuary. And when he did take his place on the platform, it was with a look of distinct discomfort on his face.

It made me begin to worry. Until he opened his mouth up there at the pulpit.

His first words to the congregation were, "I'm soaked from my tie to my socks. I'm going to get Phil for this!"

What he hadn't known before but definitely knew now was that the waders in question had been in Phil's attic for quite some time—and had dry-rotted. They were filled with tiny pinholes so that, when he stepped into the water, they filled right up, soaking his clothes and making it difficult to lift his legs.

Hearing that, all I could picture in my comical mind was him looking like a cartoon character that resembled a sprinkler. No matter that the sermon commenced, I couldn't get my mind on it, too tickled thinking of him in his wet tie, shirt, underwear, pants, and socks. Giggling and snickering in not-your-average-preacher's-wife fashion, I pretended to be doing anything but looking at him from start to finish.

After the service and everyone was gone, we walked back upstairs to the changing room, and there were his waders. He gingerly picked them up, walked to the baptistery and turned them upside down for water to gush out.

Naturally, that had me laughing all over again. And when he relayed the story to his accidentally offending best buddy, we all couldn't help but crack up some more. But the next time my husband baptized someone, you'd better believe he was prepared!

Chapter 10

Never Lost

I've shared some of my many experiences with you that were humorous, and I do hope you enjoyed them. That was definitely one of my goals with this book.

Another was to let you see that preacher's wives are human, and we do experience joys, sorrows, heartaches, pains, insecurities, and failures at times. My life as one has been very fulfilling, teaching me to totally rely on God for every need in my life and to pray daily for my husband as he ministers to people from all walks of life.

It's my genuine privilege to go to God's throne of grace every day to pray for strength to help him do the work he needs me to do in his ministry. Because strength is most definitely required when life isn't always a barrel of laughs. I've had my fair share of those reminders, including after we'd just retired.

Moving to our new home, we were getting accustomed to the mountains and the small area's general way of life and were looking forward to settling into a church home and making new friends. Sometimes, however, our plans just don't go the way we want them to and God has to reel us back into where He wants us to be.

He has to show us that He's still controlling things in our lives if we allow Him to.

We were so wrapped up in the excitement of this new phase that I believe I lost sight of God's continuous presence for a time. Then my husband woke up at four in the morning, telling me his shoulder was hurting—that, probably, he'd slept on it in some wrong position. I massaged it for a while until I heard a light snore and knew he'd fallen back to sleep.

The problem seemed solved until seven o'clock when he woke up again to say that he needed to go to the hospital because of chest pains. That and his shoulder or arm was hurting.

I immediately leapt from the bed, threw on some clothes, and wanted to call 911. But he refused to do that. No matter how many times I insisted, he said he'd be fine. In fact, being the macho, strong Marine that he still thinks he is at times, he told me he would drive.

Out of habit and knowing time was of the essence, I let him, though all I could see in my mind was him having an extreme pain and us driving off the mountain. But I couldn't bring myself to have him pull over so I could get behind the wheel because we had to get to the hospital *fast!* Praying for God's help and guidance, and especially for His peace, I desperately needed to feel His presence during the drive to the emergency room.

We did arrive safely, and they immediately began to run tests on him as soon as he explained his symptoms: shivering, clammy, chest pains, and pain in the shoulder and arm. Throughout this, I just kept thinking. Thinking and thinking and thinking.

Being new to the area, we didn't know anyone. I had no support system and, for the first time, I felt totally alone. All the questions ran through my mind.

What if he dies?

What will I do?

Who do I call to help?

All our friends and family were eight hours away or more. I didn't even know a funeral home to call if he should die. I didn't know any preachers to call either, since we'd only been visiting various churches so far.

It was a feeling of complete desperation, fear, and total separation from everyone and everything I knew. I kept begging God to give me peace and calm my nerves—to tell me what to do.

When I was able to calm down enough to make some sense of the situation, I called our church family from his previous pastorate. They immediately got the word out to the congregation so that more prayers than mine were being lifted to the throne of God.

That's when a calmness began to overtake me, and I was able to think clearly.

Nurses and doctors kept coming in and out of the room, but I no longer felt any fear. I was able to put complete trust and faith in my Lord and the vessels He was using in the field of medicine. So I was already calm when the report came back that he hadn't had a heart attack. It was pneumonia in one of his lungs, something they could treat with antibiotics. They wanted to keep him in the hospital overnight and continue to do blood work to be absolutely sure it wasn't his heart.

Trials always seem to happen when you least expect them and when you have other plans that require your presence. This was one of those times for me.

I had obligated myself to a book signing at a local bookstore several months before we moved. Not wanting to cancel and cause any inconvenience for them, I wrestled in my mind as to what to do. But my husband, now showing some progress, insisted that I go. As he pointed out, the event would only last three hours.

However, there was another issue at play besides my wanting to be with him. Only being there about five weeks, I hadn't yet driven the mountain roads into town — or anyplace else. So I wasn't familiar with store locations — or anything. And while my husband tried his best to tell me how to get back home to change and then find the bookstore downtown, I was frantic which made it hard to pay attention. I tried not to let it show, but inside, I was spazzing out.

After assuring him I could find my way, I left the hospital and mentally traced my path home. Successfully! Feeling proud that I'd arrived safely, I dressed up and went back to the hospital until it was time to go.

All was well. My confidence was now soaring.

The book signing went well, too; and, by the time it was over, I was sure I could find my way back to the hospital again for a quick visit before going home for the night. Yet, setting off, I became a bit nervous since it was now dark and I was having difficulty reading all the signs.

Thinking I was supposed to go straight, I headed in what I thought was the right direction, only to drive far enough to figure out I was lost. Between the darkness of the night and the unfamiliar mountain roads and curves and no houses to be seen anywhere, I was becoming more and more frightened. After all, I was a woman, alone on the road after dark. I didn't know what to do, with no one to call and no houses to drive to and ask for help. So I began to call out to the Lord.

To be more accurate, I began screaming out to the Lord. "Help me, God! I'm lost, and I don't know what to do!" It sounded pretty much like a person who is lost spiritually and crying out to God for salvation.

I continued to cry and scream, as if God needed me to raise my volume for Him to hear. The tears were falling, and I was having more difficulty seeing the curvy roads. And there were still no houses in sight and no human help to be found. Yet in the midst of all that, I finally began to ask for God's calmness to come over me: to give me peace and assurance that He was with me and wouldn't leave me stranded in unfamiliar territory. And so, slowly but surely, that same faith I'd drawn on at the hospital just hours before, written about in my first book, and the faith I lived by once again grew into a reality for me.

Fear and faith are totally incompatible. Fear drives out faith just as much faith drives out fear. So which was it going to be for me? I had to draw on my trust in God to see me through this.

As I began to relax and wait upon Him, I saw, out in the middle of nowhere, a small convenience store. Not knowing who would be in there or if they would help, I sat in my car, wiping at my remaining tears.

Then, all of a sudden, a lady walked out.

I immediately got out and asked if she could please tell me how to get to the hospital, and she was kind and very helpful. With the directions she provided, I soon found my way back to my husband's bedside.

Psalm 138:1 (MEV) says, *I will praise You, O LORD, with all my heart; before the gods I will sing Your praise.* Isn't it funny how we make promises to God in prayer when we're afraid or when we

want something? "God, do this for me, and I promise I will —"?
I know *I* do, and I know I probably did that night when I was
lost on the mountain roads. *God, if You'll just get me back to my
husband's bedside, I'll never travel alone again at night!*

We don't always keep our promises to God, but He always
keeps His promises to us. Hebrews 13:5 tells us that He'll
never leave or forsake us. That's a promise we can cling to in
all situations in our lives. And for that promise, I'm eternally
grateful.

Thanks be to God who will never betray His Word.

Thanks be to God who asks us for sacrifices in our lives
with every — reliable — intention of repaying us with His grace.

Thanks be to God who demands our faith and nothing
more, yet rewards us with His eternal presence and unceasing
love.

There is no doubt in my heart that, when God makes a
promise, He will keep it forever. I don't have to worry, fret,
wonder, or be disturbed over situations. He's always with me.

Chapter 11

Giving Thanks

L et's go back to Psalm 138:1 for a moment and contemplate its beautiful reminder. *I will praise You, O LORD, with all my heart; before the gods I will sing Your praise.* How often do we stop each day to sing His praise? To give thanks for all the blessings in our lives?

We have so very much to be thankful for, so never forget to offer up your thanksgiving to God.

That's not always easy, I know. It's far too simple to focus on what we don't have, don't need, or don't want. Our gratitude goes out the window.

NOT YOUR TYPICAL PASTOR'S WIFE

Yet when we open our hearts and minds to focus on gratitude, we open up a treasure of good just waiting to overflow into our lives. A grateful person knows that, by giving thanks, he or she is given even more to be thankful for.

That night when I was lost, I was so grateful that God was willing to go before me to prepare the way. I was completely at His mercy, and there was nothing I could do without His presence there with me. But here's the thing: He was there all the time!

I have learned that I still need to stop and ask Him to lead the way before I even take that first step. Otherwise, I'll stumble over the dark, hard stones I sometimes create for myself. Put simply, everything just goes more smoothly when we allow the Lord to get involved in our situations—giving us even more reason to be grateful!

So what are you thankful for? If we would all slow down long enough to take inventory of our lives and the blessings we have every day, I think we'd be surprised at just how much God does for us. In my own personal life, I'll give thanks for the smallest of things, like finding my eyeglasses or finding that paper with those important dates written on it. I know those might sound frivolous, but God specializes in hearing the little things just as much as the monumental requests we make. Plus, He always loves to hear from us, and giving thanks is a great way to stay in touch.

When was the last time you thanked Him for the night's rest you got or the fact that He opened your eyes the next morning? That you were able to walk, hear, see, taste, and feel? There are so many little things we take for granted every day, but we can change that right now.

Stop a second to Give Him thanks and praise!

If you've ever wondered if pastors' wives ever worry or complain, I can only speak for myself. In which case, the answer is emphatically *YES*.

There were so many times I woke up and just didn't want to be involved in any of the ministry that day. I'd wake up with complaints and worries on my mind, a to-do list permanently fixed in my brain the second my eyes popped open. And from that moment forward, I would find there was no time to stop and think on anything but the long list of things I had to do for myself and for others. Sometimes, I had to just pray, "Help me, Lord, to stop and breathe."

Looking back, I should have started the morning with a list of blessings I was thankful for, making an effort to carry that gratitude with me throughout the day instead of complaining and moaning and groaning about my responsibilities. Fortunately, I have improved greatly in that area of my Christian life.

Beginning your day with gratitude, prayer, and quiet time alone with God will make your day go much more smoothly and keep your feathers far less ruffled. Deuteronomy 28:2-3 (NIV) says, *All these blessings will come upon you and accompany you if you obey the Lord your God: you will be blessed in the city and in the country.* (I certainly needed that Scripture when I was lost in the mountain country.)

Read that over again, noticing how obedience and blessings are mentioned in the same exact verse. They hold true in my life and in your life, as well.

What an awesome God we serve!

Yet not only do we complain about things, but we worry, too! The Bible tells us not to worry (see Matthew 6:25-34). To be content with what we have and where we are (see 1 Timothy 6:8). In obeying, we might find that the situation we're in is a situation meant to teach us a lesson from God.

The Bible also tells us that He will supply all our needs. He'll take care of us. He won't leave us or forsake us when we find ourselves in dire situations or everyday mishaps. In other words, stop worrying!

I know it's sometimes easier said than done, and that's because we're human. We're so easily distracted by those aforementioned to-do lists that appear so very time-consuming. And maybe they are. There have certainly been times in my life when it seemed that all I did was complain and worry about such things. I needed 30 hours a day to get everything done, and no one would help. Laundry was piling up, the house needed cleaning (I mean a serious, serious cleaning), bills needed to be paid, cards needed to be sent to those with birthdays and anniversaries, music needed to be planned for the worship services . . .

The list seemed to never end, and I would worry that I couldn't accomplish everything in a certain time frame. Moreover, the more I worried, the more frustrated I became.

Sound familiar? Oh, we know that God frowns on murmuring and complaining, but we do it anyway. We grumble about long lines in the check-out lane, long stoplights, difficult neighbors, our jobs, the weather, cantankerous family members, and our household chores. Instead of going to God and thanking Him for our blessings, we approach life with a bad attitude.

But what if we adjusted our attitudes? Well, bless your heart, we just might be happy if we did! God's Word tells us to maintain a thankful spirit, and it's well-worth the effort. So try it! Hold on to it! And let your motto be "An Attitude of Gratitude."

It's amazing what peace that can bring you.

Peace. That word can carry such varying ideas. You might describe it as a day spent at the beach. An afternoon without phone calls and to-do lists. A stress-free week. But those things, lovely as they may be, only give a temporary peace. God, meanwhile, gives us a peace that surpasses human understanding—the kind that prevails in the most difficult situations.

Only the Lord can give that tranquility even in the midst of life's storms.

Peace is God's gift to us. It's a peace we possess in situations where we see no way out. In the midst of sorrow and sickness. But it's also a peace that comes over us in joy and health, as well.

When the circumstances of my life feel like a storm is blowing through—uprooting, flooding, twisting, and burying what I've worked so hard to establish—it's easy to grow frantic. Giving in to that seemingly natural urge, I'll take it to God and tell Him how I'm feeling and how I want to be able to do something to stop it. Yet I am powerless to change the course of things that are well beyond my control.

It's only when I stop flailing and grasping like a drowning swimmer that I realize my God is holding me. He has not left me to brave this storm alone. Whatever it does to my life; whatever may be damaged, lost, or destroyed—that is also in His hands. He's the one who restores, heals, and redeems if I will only give Him time to show me His peace.

Many times, although the circumstances haven't changed, everything begins to look brighter to me through the eyes of peace.

We all need to carry that peace each day, using it as an anchor against the tumult of our lives. It's so easy to get lost in our routines and those endless to-do lists. Sometimes, it might feel as if the demands of the day are threatening to blow us off-course; but we have to hold tight to the knowledge of His strength, His power, and His majesty. If we can remember that, whatever the outward circumstances may be, peace will only be a heartbeat away.

In the first several months when my first marriage ended, I couldn't find any peace within my heart. Fear took over so strongly. It was only when I began to pray earnestly that God would give me the calmness and peace I so desperately needed that I began to recognize His presence and peace – the kind of peace that only comes from Him.

You may have experienced something similar in your life. Maybe it wasn't divorce, but you found yourself struggling with circumstances just as monumental. You knew it was completely out of your control, making you recognize that only God could help. Whatever it was, isn't it strange how we as Christians seem to struggle, complain, and try to work things out by ourselves when all we have to do is so simple: turn to God in the beginning and allow Him to work out these situations?

If we would all do that, we'd save ourselves from so much stress and worry and frustration. It's sort of like purchasing an item that has to be assembled. After hours of trying to put the thing together with no success, we finally read the directions.

Why didn't we read them first? Because we thought we could do it on our own. In the same way, if we read the directions in God's Word, we'd find that all these circumstances that seem to crop up in our lives aren't so gigantic after all.

He gives us all the instructions we need for our lives.

John 16:33 (NIV) says, *"I have told you these things, so that in Me you may have peace. In this world you will have trouble. But take heart! I have overcome the world!"*

Can I get an "A-men" or "Praise the Lord" from you, dear reader?

There are so many ways Satan can try to rob our peace. But there are so many ways we can let God sustain it. Sharing in the ministry with my husband, I sometimes found it to be a lonely life. I tried very hard not to show it around him because I knew God had him right where he needed to be, and I didn't want to hinder his ministry in any way. But sometimes, pastors' wives find themselves in a lonely place simply because they have to share their husband with the entire congregation. . . possibly even the extended family members of the congregation.

There are times when you want nothing more than to snuggle up on the sofa, eat popcorn, and watch a good movie together, but you're interrupted by a phone call that takes him right away from that precious time you'd hoped for. You're left in the house to have dinner alone, watch TV alone, and sometimes even go to bed alone while you wait for him to return from ministering. I never begrudged him any of that, but sometimes we wives just need our mate. And sometimes — maybe even a lot of the time — that's not possible in ministry.

No one prepared me for this, but I soon discovered it was something I had to accept without resentment toward him or anyone who needed his help. Loneliness can destroy your testimony if you allow it to. It can conquer your peace. So whenever I was feeling lonely, I made the decision to quit wallowing in my self-induced emotion, get up off the sofa of despair, and go do something constructive for someone.

We had a neighbor who was 95 years old, widowed, and rather feeble. John was a sweet and endearing man who was always so thankful for anything anyone did for him. So I used my temporary bouts with loneliness to prepare meals for him. It was something so small, but it brought joy to him, as well as to me.

Whenever I went over, I'd make sure to spend some time listening to him and his many colorful stories. John's hands shook with old age and his fingers were numb, making it difficult for him to handle his eating utensils. As such, I'd always cut the meat, be sure to have everything on his plate, and get his usual glass of water. Sitting at his small table, preparing to eat, he would always bow his head and give thanks.

John touched my heart in so many ways. He was always so appreciative, and when I'd leave his house to cross the street to mine, I would thank the Lord for giving me this opportunity to get out of the "mullygrubs" of my life and do something that brought joy to someone else.

If you get in those moods of loneliness, too, ask God to show you what you can do to help someone else. Make a phone call, write a "thinking of you" note to encourage someone, or visit a neighbor who is lonely and would love to have someone to talk to. We get so wrapped up in our own lives and the supposed busyness of it that we fail to take time to think of others. But thinking of others can do so much to make us forget ourselves — in the best ways possible.

Do God's work. You don't have to have a college education or theological degree to do those small things that bring happiness and take away not only your loneliness, but possibly the loneliness of someone else in the process. All you need is a willing spirit to go where, when, and how you're called.

For me, my prayer went something like this:

Lord, the angels do Your work. I want to do it, too. You made me a person, not an angel. I can't fly through time or travel the universe, but I'm willing to do whatever I can. Help me see what You want me to do and stick to Your plan.

You see, my desire is to serve others just as my husband did and still does. But I had to get myself out of the way of what he needed to do and find my own specific calling. After that, I not only found that I was much happier, but the popcorn I ate alone was still tasty, and the movie I watched was still happy. Even though I was alone with it all.

Serving is one of the reasons we're on this earth and the reason Jesus said He came. When we serve each other, we're reaching out to a larger area of service to help meet the needs of others. Service is an outward sign that we belong to God and want to do His will. True servants don't just give with their hands, but with their hearts.

As Psalm 100:2 (MEV) says, *Serve the Lord with gladness: come before His presence with singing.*

God can take any loneliness we're feeling and turn it into a song of praise to Him. So move from that area of Lonely Street and Complaining Avenue, and get busy serving others. You'll find your new address is at corner of Happiness Lane and Joyful Street.

Chapter 12

Hope, Trust, and Joy

Have you ever experienced a difficult situation? I think we all have, and when we live in difficult times, it requires us to maintain a positive, hopeful attitude about the future. I know God is supremely faithful, and I also know He expects me to show His love and hope to those who feel so uncertain and hopeless. He expects that from all His children.

It's up to us to plant seeds of hope in hearts that have succumbed to the feeling of hopelessness: those who are struggling with illness, persecution, or difficult relationships. And He expects us to apply it to our own lives as well.

The hope that comes from God is hope that has the power to sustain us when nothing around us seems the least bit hopeful. Even when nothing in our lives makes sense at all, hope is a logical and lovely option to hold onto. It's vital for our mental, physical, and spiritual health. We need to pray that the Lord will help us move into the future with a steadfast spirit, looking forward in faith and hope, and trusting in the promises He's made to His people.

Jeremiah 17:7 (NIV) is worth remembering, both in good times and bad times: *But blessed is the one who trusts in the LORD, whose confidence is in Him.* You could just as easily substitute "hope" for "trust" and "confidence."

Of course, there have been times in my life and in my Christian walk when I didn't put my complete hope, trust, and confidence in Him. It was in those times I failed miserably. My confidence in Him should never waver, but it has. It still does from time to time, and it probably will continue to do so even though I try to put complete faith and trust in the Lord.

We all fall short of His glory; we all fail and falter from time to time. But here's another blessing: We don't have to stay in that position. We can get up, we can hold our heads high, and we can begin again. Otherwise, when we stay in that downtrodden state, we become bitter, anxious, non-trusting, and just plain miserable. That is not God's plan for His children. It's the very opposite. Satan has great jubilation when he sees us remain miserable.

Have you ever hoped for something? Sure you have! Maybe a larger house? A smaller dress size? A day to yourself? Or maybe you've hoped for more serious things like physical healing or the restoration of your marriage.

The word "hope" gives us a positive outlook. Without it, our lives remain broken, personal dreams go unrealized, and sick hearts lose the capacity to cope. Hope tells us to hold on in anticipation and expectation – because something good is just ahead!

Things don't always happen when and where and how we want them to, I know. And sometimes, there seem to be so many reasons to grow bitter, anxious, non-trusting, and just plain miserable. But God does have a perfect plan for each of us, even when we don't see it as blatantly as we'd prefer. He knows exactly when the right time is for the blessing we need. No amount of begging, fretting, or bargaining will bring it to us one second before its time.

We have to trust God, relying on the hope we have in Him. He will certainly bring things to pass.

One recent morning, I awoke early and listened to my husband quietly breathing, complete with a slight snore. Our sweet old cat was also sleeping on the foot of the bed, both of them totally relaxed and calm and peaceful.

Quietly, I put on my robe, went downstairs and turned on the coffee, listening as it began to gurgle and sputter. I filled my "Greatest Mom in the World" cup with coffee and walked out on the deck. Even though it was still somewhat dark outside, I could see the outline of the majestic mountains beginning to peek through the clouds of mist.

In that moment, it would have been impossible for me to do anything other than praise the Lord for the beauty, the serenity, the peace, and the calm that I felt.

In the quietness of the hour, I sat there, thanking Him for all the blessings He had poured on me and my family. We are all healthy, and our children are well, happy, and serving the Lord with grateful and generous hearts. I praised Him for my grandchildren and prayed for their protection. I thanked Him over and over for my wonderful husband, who loves and serves the Lord, and gives of himself when others need him. I thanked God for my husband's love and protection for me, and how he provides for me.

While there are those moments in life we already admitted to, where life feels overwhelming and we have to work hard to recognize and cling to hope, at other times it seems amazingly simple! It's so natural to praise and thank God for the blessings and the good things in life, of which there are so many. We were created to enjoy Him!

As I looked around our yard and heard and saw the little birds providing for their young, and then large deer with their little ones romping through the grass, I could see God's creative touch in each and every living thing. It prompted me to pray and ask Him to help us all respect everything He's created, and to be ready to learn from anything He wants to teach us.

Give Him thanks and praise in those good times, when life seems so well-planned and orderly, and everything just falls into place as it should. Just never forget to give Him thanks and praise Him in the hard times, too. The Bible tells us over and over that we should praise Him at all times, regardless of our circumstances or feelings. Praise Him when we're sad, lonely, troubled, disillusioned, disappointed, and when we just plain don't understand why things are happening the way they are. He still wants us to praise Him and to realize that these things won't last forever. He just might be trying to teach us something in the midst of our experiences!

Are we willing to listen?

Throughout life, just as we might struggle with hope, there are bound to be moments when it feels like the joy has gone out of our lives. We need God's reassurance that He never gives us a burden without helping us bear it.

Fortunately, we know that He doesn't. Never. He is always there to walk with us. Now, that's something to be joyful for, don't you agree? He will carry our yoke and solve the problem for us if we will only remain faithful and trust Him with all things. Amen!

I honestly believe that a Christian should be filled with joy (and a few giggles)! Our joy should show! When I accepted

Jesus Christ as my Lord and Savior at the tender age of 10, I had no idea what would transpire in my life as I grew. But I do vividly remember how excited I was in that moment. I didn't have all the answers to everything that would come along in my life (who does?), but I realized that God loved me enough to die for me and that He would stay close to me forever.

The joy and excitement I felt that day as a new Christian is the same joy I feel today, making its presence known so prominently so often. It just comes bubbling up, sort of like those deep belly-roll laughs I have from time to time.

Do you remember the little song we learned as children that says, "If you're happy and you know it, clap your hands?" If so, then you know it continues with exhortations to stomp your feet, say amen, and "do all three." I used to love singing that song, but it wasn't until I began to mature in my Christian walk that I learned how very true its words were.

Dear friend, sing that little song and then do what it says. If you're struggling with joy, I think you might feel better after you do. It's a spiritual condition that catches on quickly once we allow it in.

Do you know someone who has a spirit of joy? No matter what happens in life, he or she always has an uplifting word and a glorious smile. This person sparkles with that distinctive presence—brighter than diamonds—and it isn't surprising that people are drawn so strongly to that person. This person, whoever he or she may be, embodies Psalm 32:11 (NIV), which says, *Rejoice in the Lord and be glad, you righteous; sing, all you who are upright in heart!*

My mother was a joyful person indeed, no matter that she faced challenges like everyone else, especially in her later years. Her health, in particular, troubled her from time to time; but as a general rule, she chose to focus on the positive.

Her joyful outlook took on so many forms: She was calm, a good listener, loved to try new things, and was interested and interesting. But the main attribute I found in her was that she had a radiant spirit - a sparkly one, you might say - and that spirit was contagious. No matter who was with her and no matter how depressed or "down" the other person was, my mother could always lift their spirits.

There were so many times I would call to talk to her and ask for advice, which she always willingly gave. And so, whenever I'm told, "You're just like your mother," I consider it an enormous compliment to know I share that joy and can spread it to others.

Unfortunately, there are also just as many (or more) people who are negative. They can't see anything to be happy about, always complaining about something in their life. Yet how many of them claim to be Christians? More than we may know.

I have to be careful when I'm around people like that. It's not that I don't love them. I do. But if I let their negativity levels too close too often, it will affect my own joy.

Scripture encourages us to shine with joy about our salvation and the goodness of God. And not just any level of shining either. We should shine in such a way that it lights the pathway, leading others to Christ!

After all, Jesus said in Matthew 5:14-16 (NIV), *"You are the light of the world. A town built on a hill cannot be hidden. Neither do people light a lamp and put it under a bowl. Instead they put it on its stand, and it gives light to everyone in the house. In the same way, let your light shine before others, that they may see your good deeds and glorify your Father in heaven."*

One day, we'll rejoice in heaven. That fact alone should cause us to jump for joy!

We best feel this fruit of the Spirit when we're in God's hands, sensing His love, grace, compassion, and mercy at work in our lives. Knowing that, I believe we feel joy more often than we think. Let us count the ways . . .

Do you remember when your child was born, and you looked into those tiny eyes for the very first time? Is that not joy?

How about when you first fell in love? Or first achieved a major life goal? Or perhaps when you came back from a horrible disease or trauma? When God blesses us in those ways, surely we feel an abundance of joy!

Joy may be fleeting, but that's what makes it so precious and profound. If we were to feel it all the time, we wouldn't appreciate it when we did. And that would be tragic when it helps open our hearts to having a truly intimate relationship with God.

There can be no experience of joy without first having faith in Him. Our faith acts as a trigger that frees us from the anxieties, worries, and concerns that bog down our happiness, allowing us to be happy, to know it, and to clap our hands for joy!

Chapter 13

Somebody

There's one final topic I would like to discuss. It's not strictly a fruit of the Spirit like so much of what we've covered in these last few chapters. But it has the power to set us free if we are connected to the Vine, or the power to keep us in bondage if we pretend to emulate God's character apart from Him.

Jesus says in John 15:5-6 (NIV), *"I am the vine; you are the branches. If you remain in me and I in you, you will bear much fruit; apart from me you can do nothing. If you do not remain in me, you are like a branch that is thrown away and withers; such branches are picked up, thrown into the fire and burned."*

The topic of this chapter is forgiveness which, like the fruit of the Spirit, originates with God.

Let's face it: Friends fight. Spouses fight. Parents and children fight. It happens. Yet in my own life, whenever I fought back with angry and harsh words, I was bound to live to regret it.

Sometimes, in the heat of the moment, I say things I don't really mean. And words can hurt. Deeply. Do you recall the childhood saying we all used to repeat? Maybe some adults still say it today. It declares that, "Sticks and stones may hurt my bones, but words can never hurt me."

Popular though it may have been, words CAN and DO hurt. Worse yet, the wounds they leave can inflict scars that stick around for a long time. Knowing that, there have been many times I've prayed that the Lord would guard my words and mouth, and help me respond carefully with as much love and compassion as I can muster.

It's like the T-shirt I once saw that read, "Lord, put Your arm around my shoulder and Your hand over my mouth." Ha! If only.

Sometimes that is exactly what we need. Because when we're careful about what we say, giving it lots of thought first, we would doubtlessly have to ask for forgiveness a lot less.

Forgiveness doesn't come easy for some people, and yet, Jesus tells us we're to practice exactly that. Certainly, we're supposed to ask Him for forgiveness when we sin. In the Lord's Prayer, it says, *"Our Father, who art in heaven . . . forgive us our debts"* (Matthew 6:9-12 ASV). It's a request He's more than willing to grant whenever we come before Him with humble hearts. God is so very faithful in His forgiveness toward us.

Personally, I find it easy to ask God for forgiveness when I do things I shouldn't do. But I'll admit I find it a little more difficult at times to ask forgiveness of others. Isn't it so much easier to rationalize why we shouldn't?

"Well, you don't know what they did to me." Or, "The hurt just goes too deep."

There are so many reasons—also known as excuses—we can give as to why we won't forgive. Yet the truth is, when we don't, the deadly eating worm of unforgiveness will destroy us eventually. It's a cage: a trap that only leads to more pain and misery than we've already felt.

When we forgive someone who has wronged us, however, there's a feeling of being set free.

If God is quick to forgive us whenever we approach Him, why do we withhold forgiveness toward others or others withhold forgiveness from us? Are we greater than God? Nope, and our stubbornness in the forgiveness department proves it.

I believe forgiveness can be a threefold process:

1. Seek forgiveness from God.

2. Seek forgiveness from the wronged party (actual or perceived).

3. Seek forgiveness from yourself.

First, we ask for forgiveness from God. He tells us in His Word that no one is perfect; we all sin (see Romans 3:23). Therefore, we all have to go to God and ask for forgiveness for the sin(s) we've committed. We can't possibly go to someone and ask for their forgiveness until we first go to God and seek His royal pardon.

But asking any wronged parties for their forgiveness is definitely the second step. It isn't always the easiest thing to do: to admit we've done or said something against another person. Perhaps it was just a misunderstanding or wrong perception that could be cleared up if the facts were articulated and sorted through.

We never know what their reaction will be; whether our

attempt at reconciliation will be received in a loving and kind manner, or if they will shun us and not want to discuss the situation. Worse yet, is when they are willing to discuss the situation but refuse to grant the forgiveness we're asking for.

We take a big risk in asking others for forgiveness, but I know it's a scriptural command to seek it, anyway. If the other person won't accept it, then we know we've done our part anyway by following the first and second steps.

Which means that, at this point, we must try to not dwell on it.

Instead, we move to the third step which is to concentrate on in our spiritual walk with the Lord. And perhaps that's the most difficult part, keeping in step with the Holy Spirit (see Galatians 5:25). It certainly is for me, since it involves forgiving myself for whatever offense I've caused.

Philippians 3:13-14 (NIV) says, *forgetting what is behind and straining toward what is ahead, I press on toward the goal to win the prize for which God has called me heavenward in Christ Jesus.* In other words, Paul forgave himself and reached forward to better things.

This doesn't mean that Satan doesn't try to bring up our past: things we've done to hurt others or even things others have done to us. Reminding us of offenses is a dirty trick because nursing grudges is so effective. When those thoughts pop into our minds, it can be very difficult to rid ourselves of them. That's why Satan loves nothing more than to throw the past in our faces. And, if we aren't careful, we'll fall right into his hands to wallow in self-pity and make ourselves miserable over sins and mistakes that God has already forgiven.

So, when the devil does that, we must immediately think on the things of Christ and remind Satan that God has forgiven whatever incident is being used as a weapon against us. We have to remind him that the power of darkness no longer has a hold on us. This isn't always easy, but it is possible.

It's always possible.

Forgiveness requires understanding on our part.

According to Luke 23:34a (NIV), *Jesus said, "Father, forgive them, for they don't know what they are doing."* So, since we don't want to be permanently lumped in with such a crowd, we must try to understand that, in that particular moment, whoever was doing the hurting might not have been fully aware of the hurt being tossed out. As such, use some understanding when talking with them about how you felt.

This requires the intention to be merciful, something I know God has granted me so many times when I didn't deserve it. He's shown compassion and forgiveness. And, to me, the best part of all is that He won't remember those things I did that hurt someone.

Hebrews 10:17 (NIV) reminds us, *"Their sins and lawless acts I will remember no more."* That's something to praise Him for! Oh, sure, they'll crop up in my mind because Satan does things like that. But God won't remember them. Nor will He ever bring them to my remembrance. We do that to ourselves.

The highly respected 19th century preacher Charles Spurgeon once said, "When you bury a mad dog, don't leave his tail above the ground." That really struck me as poignant. When it comes to forgiveness, you need to bury everything related to what you're asking to be forgiven over. All the sins, the hurt, the pain, the embarrassment, the tears. All of it. Bury it deep, and don't dig it up!

I believe I've spent more time writing on forgiveness than any other part of this spiritual walk, but that's because it's so imperative that we practice it in our lives. We do things every day that possibly hurt others, sometimes completely cluelessly, too. That's one of the many reasons to stay so close to the Lord and so in tune with His voice: so that we are extremely careful when we speak and about what we allow to come from our hearts to our mouths.

Just remember that there's no sin beyond the scope of God's forgiveness. His blood cleanses us from all that filth, and if you've nailed your iniquities and shame to the cross, He has not only forgiven you but provided a basis for self-forgiveness as well.

There's nothing we can do to change our past. All we can do is start where we are and go forward. So live a life of faithfulness, hope, joy, praise, and thanksgiving! Let God lead you where He wants you to go, never forgetting that if He leads you to it, He'll lead you through it.

In case you face some situation that doesn't make you happy and fulfilled, just remember how He will lead you to a place of joy and completion in your life if you just let Him. Trust Him. Love Him. Live for Him, always being sensitive to the needs of others and allowing Him to use you wherever and whenever you're needed.

Enjoy your life in Christ! Laugh often and share your humor and joy with everyone. God made you to revel in His goodness.

God made you. Period.

So as I recall that child's response on the phone so many years ago, saying, "It's nobody. It's just the preacher's wife," I know beyond a shadow of a doubt that I am somebody. I'm a child of the King, for which I am eternally grateful.

And I know He wants the same for you.

Living on Faith
and Baked Potatoes

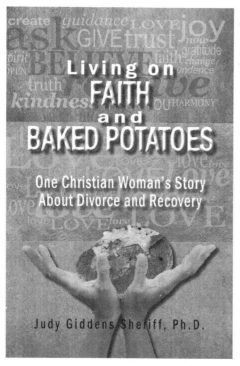

Judy opens her life to her readers in her first book, a revealing personal account of divorce and recovery. *Living on Faith and Baked Potatoes* will:

- Give you a deeper understanding of the total emptiness associated with many divorcees.

- Make you laugh, cry, and draw you into a deeper knowledge of God's continual love and acceptance of you.

- Show you how you can make it through your own separation and divorce by trusting God for His will to be completed in your life.

- Give you the assurance that God is still in control and YOU ARE NOT ALONE!

In *Living on Faith and Baked Potatoes,* Judy freely shares the intimate feelings she experienced and the coping skills she developed during the most trying period of her life. Many of us give little thought to the fact that a divorcee must quickly come to grips with the reality of continued daily living. Let Judy show you how through her humor and candor.

Not divorced? Know someone who is? This work of love is sure to become a coveted reference for those seeking to understand how they can minister to someone who is trying to put their life back together when a marriage ends. For professional counselors who are seeking a better understanding of the physical and emotional trials associated with separation and divorce, this book will be a valuable resource.

142

Meet the Author

Judy Sheriff is a retired educator with a Ph.D. in Christian Counseling who does extensive counseling with people going through separation and divorce. Judy teaches divorce recovery workshops and is available for group seminars on the subject. She enjoys speaking at women's conferences and has been the keynote speaker on numerous occasions. She is also an accomplished musician and has served as church organist, pianist, and choir director. She received degrees from Mars Hill University, Greenwich University, and Newburgh Theological Seminary. Judy and her husband, Richard, both natives of North Carolina, enjoy singing as a ministry outreach. She has two children and four grandchildren.

To schedule seminars, speaking engagements, or singing events, contact Judy at judygiddenssheriff@gmail.com.

Order Info

Available on Amazon.
For autographed copies
or to schedule seminars, speaking engagements,
or singing events,
contact Judy at
judygiddenssheriff@gmail.com.

Fruitbearer Publishing, LLC
P.O. Box 777, Georgetown, DE 19947
302.856.6649 • FAX 301.856.7742
www.fruitbearer.com • info@fruitbearer.com

Made in the USA
San Bernardino, CA
20 December 2018